Life Inside Out

A Practical and Inspirational Guide to Dealing with Cancer and Other Life-threatening Illnesses

Lyn Densem-Chambers

This book is dedicated to
my aunt Jo Miller
and my mother-in-law
Ethel Marie Chambers,
two special and beloved ladies
whose lives ended far too soon
because of cancer.

Contents

Acknowledgements

So many people helped to make this book possible that I will undoubtedly miss thanking some of them. I hope they know who they are and will recognize the fruits of their efforts in these pages.

Most of all, I want to thank my beloved family: husband Craig and son Ryan Chambers, who were always there to love and support me—along with my mother Penny Tennant, brother John Densem, sister Dana Jo Utter and their helpful spouses, Shirley and Tom; my father Douglas Densem; Evelyn Chambers and Doug Chambers; Kelly Storms; and my Colorado family, Marcie and John Smith, and Tom, Eleanor, and Bill Pangborn. I love you all!

Then there were the numerous friends who were always there to drive me to treatments, to stay in touch, and to keep my spirits up: Susan Clarke, Susie DePrez, Laura and Dave Hansen, Hannah Harris, Art and Vickie Weeast, Linda Williams, and all my lovely neighbor friends; plus the many others, from near and far, who called, visited, sent cards, flowers and emails, brought food, and always kept me in their thoughts and prayers. Although there are too many to name here, I send a special thanks to my Indian friends, Vinay and Preeti, for their Hindu blessing ceremonies and caring, and to Patty Kersey and my many other Catholic friends and relatives who regularly sponsored masses in my name. I know these helped.

Another special thanks to fellow cancer survivors Marjory Beal and Cathie Hufford for poring over my manuscript and offering helpful suggestions; also to Dottie Lamm, my husband

Acknowledgements

Craig, my son Ryan, my publishing consultant Randy Perkins, editor Claire Nagle, and designer Susan Clarke for their valuable input. It truly takes a village to sustain and nourish a book, as well as a life!

Without the caring professionalism of many healers, I wouldn't be here to write this book. They are my heroes, and I owe them my life. Thank you is an inadequate phrase, but I say it anyway:

Dr. Edward B. Arenson, MD, Mary Pierick, RN, and the staff of Colorado Neurological Institute, Englewood, Colorado

Dr. John Nichols, MD, and his staff at Intermountain Neurosurgery, Denver, Colorado

Dr. Daryl Y. Makishi, MD, DO, and the staff of Swedish Medical Center Radiology, Englewood, Colorado

Summit County Ambulance Service, Frisco, Colorado

Red White and Blue Fire/Rescue, Breckenridge, Colorado

St. Anthony Summit Medical Center and Flight for Life, Frisco, Colorado

The nurses and emergency staff of St. Anthony Central Hospital in Denver, Colorado

Dr. Susan Papner, DO, Englewood Family Physicians, Englewood, Colorado

My healing process has involved other caring professionals, as well: Thank you to Drs. Richard Damiano, Lance Forstot, Erik Letko, and the staff of Corneal Consultants of Colorado, who have never given up on helping me regain sight in my shingles-damaged eye; and to the lovely massage therapists of Medicine Hands of Colorado—Joyce Wanderer, Cheryl Johnson, Annie Cotton, and Jan Wilson—who selflessly volunteered untold hours to helping me and other cancer patients feel better during the healing process; and to the many alternative health practitioners who continue to treat and advise me in my journey toward ongoing health, providing helpful content for this book along the way.

Preface

Before cancer disrupted my life, I was an ordinary person with a family, a profession, and every expectation of living a long, normal life. That expectation changed suddenly and dramatically right before Thanksgiving 2005, with an emergency Flight for Life helicopter ride from the Colorado mountains to St. Anthony Central Hospital in Denver, where surgeons removed a bleeding, cancerous tumor from my head.

For the first time, I came face to face with my own mortality, and little has been "ordinary" about my life since. Fifty-eight and, to all appearances, in excellent health, I was unexpectedly forced to consider the very real possibility of imminent death. Like so many cancer patients and others diagnosed with a deadly disease, I could no longer take life for granted.

Thus began the first steps of my journey dealing with a life-threatening illness, a very deadly and rare form of brain cancer called Glioblastoma Multiforme, or GBM. An experience unlike any I had ever had was about to begin. The next three years of my life would be consumed with doctor visits, hospital tests, radiation, and chemotherapies, sprinkled with tears and fears, yet wrapped in hope and love. I have learned more about life and myself "A.D." (After Diagnosis) than in all the other years of my life "B.C." (Before Cancer). What I learned helped me rise to the challenge of this frightening disease.

During this turbulent period, I kept a journal of my thoughts, discoveries, inspirations, and the techniques that helped me stay strong. I also used this new-found time to educate myself about cancer and wellness.

Today I am a cancer survivor who has completed several years of intensive treatment. Encouraged by my good fortune and positive attitude, other cancer patients and their friends have asked me to share my experience.

Unfortunately, my experience is not unique. Cancer diagnoses are rising at an alarming rate throughout the world. In fact, the rate is growing so rapidly that the World Health Organization predicts global cancer deaths could double by 2030.[1] In just one year, I was contacted by eleven friends or friends of friends who had been diagnosed with cancer, including four with GBM! I began to wonder if my unwelcome cancer education could be helpful to others on a larger scale. So, using my personal journal as a guide, I started to record and research the ideas and techniques that sustained me through cancer, a time when my life was turned inside out.

Life Inside Out is a practical and inspirational guide for anyone dealing with a life-threatening illness, from patients to family and friends. Practically, it contains information and suggestions for meeting the everyday challenges of diagnosis, treatment, and prevention. Inspirationally, the book is woven with personal thoughts and quotations from a few of my favorite philosophers and spiritual leaders.

The book focuses on cancer, but the basic concepts also apply to other life-threatening illnesses that prey on a weakened immune system. For example, those diagnosed with heart disease or diabetes may go through similar stages of adjustment and benefit from the wellness information contained in these pages.

Although *Life Inside Out* is based on my personal experience, it includes information from other sources, both anecdotal and research-based. I am not an expert in the areas I explore, but I am an expert in what it feels like to navigate the stormy sea of cancer. I hope others on a similar course will find inspiration, practical assistance, and, most of all, hope in the following pages.

Note: This book is not a comprehensive reference for "all things cancer." Rather it is meant to serve as a general guide and initial resource for further research in areas of interest to the reader. Decisions on individual courses of action should ultimately be made by the patient and his or her medical advisors.

A family Christmas photo, taken one month after surgery
and diagnosis. My husband Craig, son Ryan, and me.

Chapter 1:

My Story

> *When all that has been ordinary is suddenly wiped from your life, your life suddenly becomes EXTRAordinary.*
> *— Lyn*

There were no obvious early symptoms of the poison developing in my head. Yes, I had been irritable and stressed in the previous several months. But that didn't seem striking, given the fact that I was in the process of leaving a beloved job for unknown territory. After five years as the director of an international exchange program, I had decided it was time to move on. To where, I didn't know, and I'm sure this was part of my stress.

My husband Craig had long been concerned about my persistent headaches and had urged me to check on them early in our marriage. However, I had always dismissed them as symptoms of sinus problems and stress. Would things have been different if I had checked them out earlier? Doctors say probably not, but we'll never know.

On the night of November 21, 2005, I went to bed at our Colorado mountain cabin with a splitting headache that really lived up to the description. My usual headaches got worse every time we went to the mountains, so I figured it was just altitude-induced. Neither Craig nor I became alarmed by the intensity of this one. Nevertheless, it was so strong and immune to my usual doses of pain relievers that I remember pressing my fingers hard against my forehead that night before lying down to sleep, and pleading for it to be gone by morning. It wasn't!

About 5 a.m. I suddenly shot up in bed with a searing pain that sliced through my head like an ax, from the base of my neck to the top of my skull. Still asleep, I somehow made my way down the narrow stairs of our cabin loft to the bathroom below, where I succumbed to violent convulsions of nausea. Realizing that something was terribly wrong, I called up to my husband that I thought I was having a stroke.

Groggy and thinking it was just another one of my usual headaches, Craig took a few minutes to make his way down the loft stairs. But once he saw me sprawled awkwardly in the tiny bathroom, he knew this was very different.

At first he encouraged me to lie down on the living room sofa while he prepared to drive me to the nearest emergency room. However, when it became clear that I couldn't even manage the short walk to our car parked just outside the door, he called 911.

I barely recall the bustle of the emergency crews inside our tiny living room. Craig tells me he had to move furniture aside to accommodate them and their equipment. "Count backwards from ten," I remember one said, and, according to Craig, I did so without a problem, correctly answering all of the usual assessment questions. That's where my memory fades.

I don't remember the ambulance ride to the local hospital, nor the commotion and tests that quickly took place upon my arrival. Most regrettably, I don't remember the Flight for Life helicopter ride that soon whisked me to St. Anthony Central Hospital in Denver. My first helicopter ride and I missed it!

The Fight for Life

The preliminary diagnosis was that I had a bleeding mass in my brain that could send me into an irreversible coma if not immediately treated. As I flew unaware through the early morning sky to the waiting emergency room in Denver, Craig retrieved our two dogs from our cabin and quickly drove down to Denver to drop them off at home before joining me at the hospital.

En route he called our son Ryan, who had just begun his shift as a ski patroller at the nearby Breckenridge Ski Resort; Craig then called my mother, brother, and sister in Portland, Oregon. Due to the potential danger of the situation, he urged them all to come as soon as they could. My 81-year-old mother put aside her fear of flying to board a plane that afternoon, sitting stiff with terror between my sister and my brother, who claims his thumb is permanently elongated from her vice-like grip.

Ryan raced down from the mountaintop where he was completing morning preparations for opening the ski slopes. He then drove the 80 miles to the hospital in a blur, his father's warning that I would want him by me "in one piece" undoubtedly disregarded in favor of speed.

By the time Craig and Ryan arrived at the hospital, I had already been prepped for surgery. The doctor said I was deteriorating neurologically and rapidly slipping into a coma, so time was critical. I later heard how Craig and Ryan worriedly paced the waiting room during the four-hour surgery, sharing concerns that I might not make it through the operation--or, if I did, that I might never be the same, as the surgeon had warned.

Fortunately, the universe had other plans. To the surprise of everyone, including my surgeon, I awoke in the recovery room talking up a storm with a male nurse who reminded me of my son. Ryan also worked in the field of emergency medicine, and I couldn't have felt prouder of him.

Before long, Craig was cracking jokes with my surgeon about whether he had removed the part of the brain that argues with a husband. How many times had he heard that one! The relief in the room was palpable, even through my anesthesia haze.

The surgeon had performed a miracle, removing the bleeding mass as cleanly as humanly possible. But perhaps he had had some non-human help. I later found out that a prayer circle had been organized for me by a friend in Oregon during the operation. I also couldn't help but wonder about the fact that most of the nurses attending to me during and after the emergency were named Mary. I'm neither terribly religious nor Catholic, but hmm.

Diagnosis

Within a couple of weeks I was on my way to recovery from the surgery, joking with friends and family about having a hole in my head. Cards, flowers, visitors, and well-wishes from around the world flowed into the house as I made a remarkable come-back from surgery. It seemed like a fairy-tale ending to a traumatic, but temporary, turn in my life.

Unfortunately, this was no fairy tale. My husband and I were at a mall when the surgeon's nurse called with test results on the tumor. The biopsy had been delayed because of the

Thanksgiving holiday, so I was anxious to hear from her anyplace, anytime. When she asked if there was someplace I could sit down, I knew the news wasn't good. Nevertheless, I was stunned by the diagnosis: an extremely deadly brain cancer, Glioblastoma Multiforme. Grade Four.

I soon learned that, unlike in school, a higher grade isn't better for tumors. Four is the worst, and, as a comedian once joked, there is no five! I later found out that GBMs are also quite rare: Generally, less than 15,000 cases of GBMs are diagnosed annually in the U.S., compared to more than 200,000 cases each of breast and prostate cancer.[2] It is the same kind of tumor that killed Senator Edward (Ted) Kennedy and journalist Robert Novak. It gave me no sense of pride to be in such rare company.

I went through the typical stages of grief: anger, denial, depression, and, finally, acceptance. Yet it was a voice inside my head reassuring me that everything was going to be all right that got me through the initial pain. Was this just wishful thinking? Regardless, a spirit of survival was moving into that newly vacated space in my brain. I had an intuitive sense that I was going to make it through this just fine. But what happens now? I wondered.

The Journey Begins

The next few weeks were a hectic blur–consulting with numerous doctors to find the best course of action, the magic exit from this nightmare. I hoped against hope that one of the doctors would assure me that there was an instant cure. Just take two aspirin, go to bed, and everything will be fine in the morning. It was a very lonely and confusing time.

Thus began my journey dealing with a life-threatening disease. It would be a long and difficult trip—more than three years of aggressive radiation, chemotherapy, and biological drugs that would sap me of energy, make me lose my hair, and expose me to other ailments that capitalize on immune system suppression.

Family, friends, and prayer helped me through this challenging time. I also read, talked to experts, and sought all the support I could find. In the process, I discovered common experiences, concerns, and qualities that cancer survivors share. I decided to summarize them in a simple and easy-to-use book to help other cancer patients and their supporters.

The following pages are based on the journal I kept during my encounter with cancer, reflecting what I thought and learned from this unexpected side-trip through life. They contain practical information and advice, interspersed with inspirational thoughts and quotations. Each chapter contains tips on useful information.

I hope this book will help those facing cancer or other life-altering diseases. I also hope it inspires others never to take life for granted and to enjoy its gifts every moment of every day.

I wrote this poem earlier in the year in which my tumor was discovered, on a trip to the Oregon Coast with my mother. I wondered later if my unusual discomfort with the ocean I had always loved so dearly was a premonition of the stormy seas to flood my life eight months later.

Premonition

I walk along the dark morning beach
    with just a left-over moon
        to light my way.
            Its beacon shimmers
            on the fingertips of shallow waves
                that gently brush the shore.
            I am alone in this magic space
                where the ocean taps the shoulder of the earth,
                where all things are both possible
                and terrifying.
In the wake of tsunamis that exposed
        the ocean's angry power,
        the once peaceful solace of the sea
            foams anxious in my soul
                as I feel my footing
                    along the hardened edge
                    of the shallow surf.
The sea has abandoned me,
        like a lonely piece of driftwood,
            wondering
                what the next wave will bring.

Life Inside Out

Chapter 2:

Dealing with Diagnosis

Journal entry one week after diagnosis:
   As I recall the trauma and grace of the past weeks, it strikes me that, other than feeling incredibly blessed to be alive, I am little different today than before. Actually, I am much better off, because, had this emergency not occurred, I would not have been aware of the danger living inside me and able to do something about it.
   Life is so fragile and can change at any minute for anyone. All it takes is a wrong step across a busy street, an innocent drive through an intersection, or a heart attack after jogging. The difference for me is that I know the Reaper who threatens at this moment, and I have a chance to disarm him.

A New Reality

When I first awoke from the anesthesia and to the yet-undefined reality of what had happened, I was full of wonder and gratitude for the amazing acts of skill and heroism that had yanked me from the edge of death. Once the full story emerged to my understanding, I continued to be buoyed by the love and support of family, friends, doctors, and nurses.

Cards, flowers, calls, emails, and visits from friends engulfed me in a warm embrace for weeks after I left the hospital. They gently eased me back to life, if not reality. As someone who had been through a similar experience put it, it was like being present at one's own funeral.

However, this post-crisis euphoria was soon cut short by the results of my biopsy. Cancer. The Big C—that dark fear that lurks in the shadows of every mammogram, Pap smear, prostate exam, and colonoscopy, like a childhood monster hiding under the bed. Now the monster had become real, appearing large and menacing to change my dreams into nightmares.

I was suddenly mortal. Death was no longer a hazy concept pushed to the farthest reaches of my consciousness. According to statistics, I could die within months. Not decades or years, but as few as six to eighteen months. My life was suddenly being quantified and crammed into a cold, ugly, statistical box.

What would happen to the unfulfilled dreams that had always lined my path like trees disappearing over the horizon? With diagnosis came the stark realization that I would be sidetracked from the itinerary I had planned for my life. I had always expected to live well into my nineties, like my grandparents; and my longtime focus on health had left no room for thoughts of vulnerability. Mortality. Death. A very new reality had emerged.

But surely this was just a brief detour from my path, an inconvenience that would soon be resolved. After all, I was in control of my life, right? Always the achiever, the planner, the one in charge, I was suddenly vulnerable. Something beyond me had taken over, and the only recourse I had now was how I dealt with it. Losing control is hard for someone accustomed to thinking she had it.

It took a few weeks before I realized that this disease and all its accessories--decisions, emotions, physical burdens, and lifestyle changes—presented a challenge more daunting than any I had ever encountered. I realized that the personal identity forged through job titles, accomplishments, and honors wields no clout against one's mortality. What good are titles and awards in fighting disease? In the end, we are all emperors with no clothes. The most important titles I had now were mother, wife, daughter, sister, friend, and human being.

The worth of past accomplishments would only be found in how well they had helped forge my strength of spirit, ability to learn, and resilience. Relationships past and present would form a foundation to encourage and sustain my spirit.

Everything would be fine, my inner voice told me. I could do it. And so I would. Not, however, without a lot of help, determination, and good fortune.

Letting Go

Journal entry ten days after diagnosis:
Today it really hit me. Full force. And I finally cried. In the shower, so it wouldn't show. I know it's important to mourn in order to move on. I don't want this new life!

Yet I am grateful that I have life. And I'm determined to move through and past these current "inconveniences" to a better self and greater fulfillment. Perhaps my stubborn personality will be an asset after all.

When learning any new sport or skill, experts say it is important to let yourself go before you can get "in the zone" of being at one with the goal. I remember how true that was when I first got the knack of snow skiing: I had to let go of my fears, stop watching the ground beneath me, and let my body flow toward the horizon. So it was with learning how to deal with cancer.

At first, I kept looking down, trying to maintain control and make it all go away. In retrospect, I can see that my husband was right when he said I was going through the traditional stages of grief: denial (This can't be happening!), anger or self-pity (Why me? It's not fair!), bargaining (I'll do anything if I could just live long enough to . . .), depression (Nothing is the same; why bother caring?), and, eventually, acceptance (It's going to be okay, one way or another. I'll make it through this.)[3]

Do these emotions sound familiar? If so, it may help to know that you are not alone, and it is a perfectly natural process you are going through. Many books have been written to help people move through the grieving process. I have listed a few references at the end of this book.

For me, coming to terms with reality took prayer, meditation, talking with loved ones, journaling, and reading self-help books like this one. But I won't deny sobbing in the shower or the wakeful nights and fits of anger when no one was looking. I remember staring at a movie my husband and I had rented and not seeing any of it, lost in a deep, forlorn sadness about the cruel turn of events that now overshadowed my existence.

I was fortunate to have many loving family members, friends, and acquaintances to help me through this trying time. I will forever be indebted to them for their kindness in calling, visiting, sending messages, flowers, and food. These were therapeutic in ways they may never understand. Many of the cards, plants, and gifts still decorate my home, as ongoing reminders of the wonderful people from near and far who sent them.

Due to my career in the international field, the reminders were eclectic— good luck charms from my Chinese friends, e-mails from my Muslim friends, crucifixes and mass cards from my Catholic friends, offerings from Hindu healing rituals performed by my Indian friends, a painted gourd from an

African friend, and inspirational sayings from my religiously uncommitted friends. Years directing an international exchange program added a profusion of multicultural blessings to my convalescence.

Tips for Dealing with Diagnosis

Acknowledge your feelings. They are normal, and most people go through stages of grief before they are able to accept this cataclysmic shift in their lives. So cry, scream, pray, talk with others, or start a journal of your feelings, but don't keep your emotions bottled up inside. The resulting stress isn't helpful for regaining your health.

Get counseling, if needed. Doctors, social services, and religious institutions can recommend confidential counselors to help you process and deal with your emotions. These services are often free or covered by insurance. Do not hesitate to ask for help at this difficult time. Encourage family members to do so as well.

Keep in mind that you are not a statistic, and there is always hope. Avoid checking Internet statistics about your diagnosis until after you have talked to your doctor. Statistics do not take into account your individual situation, and every case is unique.

Contact others with a similar diagnosis who can empathize and offer you hope. Cancer can be a lonely journey that only those who have traveled it truly understand. If you can't locate other cancer survivors on your own, check with your doctor, the American Cancer Society, or websites that feature chat rooms about cancer survival. The key word here is "survival." Seek people or resources with success stories or a positive approach.

Allow others to help you. Accepting support is not a sign of weakness, but of strength: It is often more difficult to accept help than to give it. However, it is important to understand that loved ones and friends also must deal with feelings regarding your diagnosis, and it may help them to help you.

Surround yourself with a positive environment—people and things that inspire you. Avoid negative influences as much as possible. This includes negative people, situations, or places—anything that brings you down instead of up.

Take one step at a time. Forget six months from now, or two years, or five. Every process consists of individual steps made one by one. That's doable. And that's real. Remember, "The past is history; the future is a mystery, and the present is a gift."

Focus on the moment. Appreciate the small details of everyday life: the way the sun casts a shadow across the floor, the texture of a curtain, the smell of a flower, a baby's smile. We miss so many moments of life in our busy-ness. This is a time to stop and, literally, smell the roses. You may be amazed at how much peace this brings.

Seek spiritual strength through prayer, meditation, or whatever means fits your beliefs. Numerous studies indicate that spiritual beliefs and practices can have a positive effect on physical and emotional health.[4]

Take care of yourself. Do what makes you feel good; take some time off work, if possible; or continue to work at a slower pace if time off is not an option; eat what appeals to you, unless you have dietary restrictions. (A note for chocolate lovers: A moderate amount of dark chocolate has actually been shown to have healthy effects on the mind and body.[5]); nap when needed; get a massage (Oncology clinics sometimes offer this as a free service to help relieve patients' discomfort during therapy.); participate in light exercise if you feel up to it. Remember, you now have a new full-time job—getting well.

Prepare yourself for a "new normal." Don't expect your life to be what it used to be. You will experience physical, emotional, and mental changes both during and after treatment. Some of these changes will be permanent and become a "new normal" for your life. Some will be physically and mentally challenging; some will make you a better person, with a deeper appreciation for life; but, bottom line, you will not come out of this experience the same person you were before.

Life Inside Out

Chapter 3:

Making Decisions

Journal entry two weeks after diagnosis:
   My mind floats back to childhood as I review my life to seek answers... "The Shadow" menaces from the bedroom radio as I cuddle on the bed with my mother, brushing her long ponytail. Then I am standing in a dried-up mud puddle in the middle of the street, where I got my first kiss at age six, and where another little girl was later shot in the eye with a B-B gun...I remember how I envied the boy down the hill who got to eat ice cream for a week after he had his tonsils taken out. And how I first learned about death when the young girl down the street died of leukemia. Life's lessons began early. And now I have one of my own, bigger than anything I could ever have imagined those many years ago.

Choosing a Doctor and Treatment Program

Finding the right doctors and treatment program for your needs can be a daunting process. Unless you are enrolled in an HMO or PPO with a predetermined range of choices, you are not likely to have oncologists, radiation technicians, and surgeons already selected. You may need to rely on recommendations from other doctors or friends.

   My introduction to cancer resulted from emergency surgery, so fate made the choice of surgeon for me. I was fortunate to land (literally!) with an excellent one, Dr. John Nichols at St. Anthony Central Hospital. In fact, without his amazing skill and expertise, I wouldn't have survived to choose any doctors.

My surgeon, therefore, was the one to give me my diagnosis and suggest choices for an oncologist. He recommended two well-regarded doctors located in the area where I live. Secretly hoping for a different diagnosis, I also sought opinions from health care professionals with whom I had long-term relationships. I believe that was a good thing to do, despite complicating my decision by expanding options. When you're scared and confused already, too many choices may be harder to deal with than too few.

Nevertheless, if you consider a variety of treatment possibilities before making a decision, you are more likely to find the best program for your unique preferences and needs. The two recommendations I got from my emergency surgeon represented very different approaches, one distinctly more aggressive than the other. Having been into holistic health for years, I also checked out a third option, a clinic that focused primarily on natural therapies.

How to choose? If you are technologically inclined, you can use the Internet to research the credentials and approaches of recommended doctors. You can also seek information directly by calling or visiting doctors' offices for free consultations. Often they will provide you with information packets about their programs. I first assembled as much information as I could about recommended doctors, then made consultation appointments with those who looked most promising.

I felt like Goldilocks tasting the three bears' porridge—one therapy was too hot (aggressively chemical), one too cold (totally natural), and one perhaps "just right" (moderately chemical). Because I wanted to minimize the use of chemical and radiological therapies, I dismissed the more aggressive option right away. On the other hand, I felt that the entirely natural approach was too risky for the kind of cancer that I had. So I initially chose the doctor with a "moderately chemical" approach.

Life, however, isn't a storybook fable, and choices aren't always that simple. My consultation with the first recommended doctor left doubts in my mind. Although he was professionally impressive, his clinic seemed impersonal. He and his staff didn't return calls on a timely basis, and the treatment centers he used were long drives from home. Nothing felt comfortable—a factor I would later come to believe is one of the most critical elements in choosing a treatment plan.

A Coincidence?

Despite my misgivings, I prepared for treatment with this first doctor. I started getting fitted for a radiation mask and made an appointment with my primary care physician, Dr. Susan Papner, for pre-treatment flu and pneumonia vaccinations. (My oncologist now also recommends a shingles vaccination, which wasn't commonly available at that time.)

Dr. Papner was quite concerned when she learned about the cancer, and she insisted that I talk to an oncologist down the hall before finalizing my treatment choice. My belief that there are no coincidences was confirmed when, ironically, this oncologist turned out to be the aggressive option that I had earlier dismissed, Dr. Edward Arenson of the Colorado Neurological Institute.

Although I was still wary of Dr. Arenson's "take-no-prisoners" approach, a quickly granted consultation was convincing. My husband and I were impressed with his record of success treating this deadly form of cancer and with his treatment program, which included patient and family support groups, free massage treatments, and optional spiritual sessions. Before we left his office, we found ourselves discussing shared interests in poetry and art, and were surprised to learn that this ostensibly traditional doctor was actually a Renaissance man with a stethoscope. We were not only persuaded by his professional approach, but by his personal warmth and dedication, traits we found shared by his top-notch staff. A sense of comfort washed over us, and we knew we had made our choice.

Even so, I studied the program notebook that the doctor had provided and talked to one of his willing patients before making a final commitment. I wanted to make sure my emotional and intellectual selves were in sync. This was, after all, one of the most important decisions of my life.

I believe I made the right choice. Three years of intensive chemotherapy and other therapies yielded success in keeping the cancer at bay. But not without cost. After my first year of treatment, I contracted shingles, a relatively common occurrence in those with immune systems weakened by chemotherapy. The disease left scars on the cornea of my right eye, resulting in blurred vision. Despite two cornea transplants and years of various treatments, at this writing my vision in that eye is still obstructed. Nevertheless, I am alive, and that is what counts!

Tips for Choosing the Right Therapy and Doctor

• **Gather as much information as you can on your type of cancer**--what it is, what causes it, and the treatment options available. Start with trusted sources like your doctors and the American Cancer Society (*www.AmericanCancerSociety.org*), then branch out to online research, books, and others who have gone through your kind of cancer.

• **Get a variety of professional opinions about your diagnosis** from healthcare professionals with diverse approaches before making treatment decisions. Each may bring a slightly different perspective to your situation. Include not only oncologists and surgeons, but also your primary care physician and any alternative healthcare providers you may have.

• **Determine your goal for treatment**: Is it complete recovery at all costs? An emphasis on quality of life? Or some of both? This, plus the severity of your diagnosis, will help you decide how aggressive your treatment should be.

• **Check out prospective doctors' training and experience** with your type of cancer. One well-respected source is the American Medical Association at *www.ama-assn.org*; however, this site only lists AMA members. If you are researching a doctor not registered there, you may need to do an individual Internet search. Careful scrutiny is especially important if you are researching doctors or clinics outside of the United States that are not required to meet U.S. regulations and standards.

• **Interview your top choices of doctors** to see if you are comfortable with their treatment philosophies and approaches. (See *Questions to Ask Prospective Doctors, page 34.*)

• **Talk to current or former patients of the doctor(s) you are considering**. Ask to be connected to one or two willing patients who can give you an honest appraisal of their experiences.

• **Consider the convenience of getting to and from treatment facilities**. This is an important factor, since you will likely be spending a lot of time at these facilities for a while.

• **Trust yourself.** Once you are aware of the pros and cons of different types of therapies and doctors, trust your instincts and go with what makes you feel the most comfortable. You know what is best for your body and mind.

Questions to Ask Prospective Doctors

❑ What are the goals and philosophy of the treatment program?

❑ What are the specifics of the treatment program?—i.e., therapies, treatment schedule, side-effects of therapies, preparations needed, facilities used?

❑ What is the success rate of the program for treating your kind of cancer?

❑ What kinds of support can you expect from the doctor and the staff?

❑ Are there services such as massage, counseling, activities and support groups?

❑ What are the costs and payment options? If you are insured, check to see if the doctor's services are covered under your plan. If you are not insured, will the doctor's office provide a payment plan or help you seek financial assistance?

❑ Are there current or past patients who would be willing to share their opinions on the program and quality of care at the facility?

Helpful Observations

During your doctor consultations, you can tell a lot by observing how staff members interact with you and each other. From your first telephone call to your first office visit, notice how they respond. Are they respectful to each other, as well as to patients? Do they return calls within 24 hours and schedule appointments for patients' convenience? Are they pleasant and do they deal with emergencies in a prompt and caring way?

Does the doctor keep appointments with reasonable punctuality? During your appointment, do you feel that the doctor takes sufficient time with you, sharing test results and different options for treatment readily and understandably? Most important, does he or she listen carefully and answer questions to your satisfaction? Remember, you are an important agent in the success of the treatment program.[6]

Journal entry three weeks after diagnosis:
The visits from friends have shrunk to just sympathy cards and calls. One phone message reminded me too powerfully of my situation, which I've wanted to push out of my mind, as if by ignoring it, perhaps I'll wake up tomorrow to find it was just a bad dream. Snuggle in with the darkness.

Finances and Insurance

Finances may play a major role in determining your treatment program. Be sure to check with the doctors you are considering about their program costs, insurance procedures, and how the office staff will help you deal with the complexities of insurance claims. The more help you get, the better. This is no time to be unnecessarily burdened with insurance worries. Your main job is to get well.

If you are no longer able to work and have a group health insurance policy with your current employer, consider taking a leave of absence rather than quitting your job. This allows you to stay insured through your employer, and, if you need to leave your job at some point, you may qualify to continue your health insurance at group rates through the Federally-mandated healthcare continuation program called COBRA.

Note: Under new Federal health insurance laws, provisions may have changed since this writing. It is advisable to seek advice from your health-insurance provider or another knowledgeable source. For more information on COBRA, check *www.dol.gov//ebsa/faqs/faq_consumer_cobra.html* .

Cancer treatments are very expensive, so I urge you to maintain healthcare coverage if you can. As a point of reference, the gross cost of my treatments has totaled nearly one million dollars since that cold November day in 2005. Without healthcare coverage, my husband and I would almost certainly have been bankrupt by now, and I may not have received the excellent care I discuss in these pages.

When I became ill, I was no longer able to work, so the major financial burdens of the household fell to my husband. Wanting to be helpful, I decided to take charge of managing insurance claims, mistakenly thinking this would be the easier task. I later learned that it can almost be a full-time job in itself, merging claims with insurance payments and figuring out actual charges owed. During the countless hours I spent wrestling with insurance claims, I learned some valuable tips that may be helpful to you:

Tips for Dealing With Insurance

• **Verify insurance coverage in advance.** Check with your insurance company *before* treatments to verify coverage and your charges. Your doctor's office may be able to help with this, since major services such as MRIs often must be pre-authorized through them.

• **Set up a file** with color-coded folders for bills "to be paid," "paid," and "to be reconciled" (those you need to verify with the insurance company). Place incoming bills into the appropriate files *as they arrive*, to make sure they don't get lost or ignored.

• **Stay on top of insurance payments as your medical bills arrive**, matching medical bills with insurance payments and EOBs (estimate of benefit statements sent to doctors and patients). Before paying a bill, make sure there are no pending insurance payments that will reduce the amount of your responsibility. A call to the insurer and the biller may save you money, if not time. Plus it could deflect credit problems for you if the insurance company is late in paying. Medical providers are sometimes willing to make adjustments to your billing due dates when they know you are trying to help them work with insurers.

• **Take notes on any conversations with insurers,** including the names of customer service representatives and any reference numbers for the call. This information is important for verifying insurance payments and benefits with your healthcare providers.

• **Retain copies of paid bills** for possible use with your taxes. At this writing, Federal Tax Code allows you to claim a percentage of your income in medical costs. Check with an accountant to see if you qualify.

• **Keep insurance ID and phone numbers handy,** both in your files and with you at all times.

Financial Assistance

Your doctor may be able to help you locate financial assistance programs, if needed. Check to see if you qualify for Medicaid. There may also be state or local assistance programs, grants, loans, or research projects to help cover uninsured costs. Plus medical offices are often willing to set up installment payment plans.

If you are unable to return to work because of your illness, you may qualify for Social Security Disability Insurance, which may also make you eligible for Medicare earlier than age sixty-five. Check with your doctor to see if you meet the criteria, and check your eligibility and benefits at *www.socialsecurity.gov*, or call 1-800-772-1213. There is a waiting period before payments can be made, so apply as early as possible.

Chapter 4:

LIVING through Therapy

> *The journey of a thousand miles starts from beneath your feet.*
> *-Tao Te Ching*

Journal entry one month after diagnosis:

I am so grateful for the caring professionalism of the amazing doctors, nurses, and emergency personnel who saved my life and allowed me to get to this point of recovery. I am also deeply grateful for the love and prayers of so many friends and family members who have provided emotional and physical support during this critical time.

Most of all, I am grateful for each day, each moment—the sunlight sprayed across the bedroom wall; the waving leaves of the backyard trees; my husband's morning kiss; the smile on my son's face in the dresser photo; the warmth of slippers on my feet ... I am newly grateful for small moments once barely noticed--just one of the unexpected gifts received in coming face to face with my own mortality.

Embracing the Challenges

Once I finally came to terms with my diagnosis, I was able to let doctors guide me to a treatment plan; allow friends and family to help in whatever ways they could; and stop grieving my losses so I could embrace my challenges.

Many people have remarked on my positive approach to dealing with this terrible disease and its side-effects. Underlying my success in staying positive then and now is a resilience built and maintained not only by the support of so many fine individuals in my life, but by a personal dedication to focusing on hope, love, and humor. There is much evidence that the mind-body connection plays an important role in healing. At the very least, a positive attitude can improve one's quality of life. Hope, love, and humor helped me stay positive, which, in turn, helped me navigate the stormy waters of my voyage through cancer. I believe these are essential lifelines for survival and peace of mind.

Hope. The best initial advice I got from my doctors was not to pay attention to statistics. Like many others newly stricken, I couldn't resist checking the Internet shortly after diagnosis. The survival rate statistics for GBM cancer were depressing. However, my doctors emphasized that each of us is unique, and statistics are based on averages and norms. We are human beings, not numbers, and there is always hope. Life doesn't come with a guarantee, so we need hope to keep us moving forward. Without it, no doctor could heal.

Hope flourishes in the stories of survivors, the exceptions to the rule, the Lance Armstrongs and the many cancer survivors I have known personally. They became my role models, replacing statistics. As aptly stated in the title of a book by Dr. Robert Buckman, *Cancer is a Word, not a Sentence.* Dr. Buckman notes the little-emphasized fact that, of all the people who are diagnosed with cancer in a year, more than half will survive and not have a recurrence. So the positive person would say the glass is more than half full!

Love. Don't underestimate the healing power of giving and receiving love. It is an essential ingredient for staying positive. This may be a time when you get back in touch with those friends you were always too busy to call, when you can bask in the glow of knowing how much you are loved and appreciated by family, friends, and even strangers.

If you are fortunate to have family and friends who want to help, accept their offers of love. This isn't always easy, especially if you're accustomed to being independent, or still in denial about your diagnosis. Some people with cancer prefer to move on and not be reminded of their situation by offers of sympathy and help.

I understand. For a while after diagnosis, I found it very difficult to see the looks of sadness on the faces of caring friends. It made me feel like an object of pity. But, most of all, it highlighted my situation, which I just wanted to forget. Experts say that denial is a necessary part of the grieving process, helping one "buy time to find the inner strength and external resources necessary to cope with traumatic loss."

After I moved past the stage of denial to acceptance and hope, I began to let go and recognize that it was okay not to be in control, that it was okay to accept help. Moreover, it was nourishing and healing. I found that it not only helped me maintain my strength and resolve, but it helped my friends and family with their own grieving and healing processes.

In our personal pain, it is easy to forget that those who care about us are also hurting. They are often fighting their own fears and feelings of inadequacy in coping with the diagnosis. In fact, they may feel even more helpless than we do, especially if they are relegated to the sidelines. Giving them ways to support us can make them feel useful and more in control of their own feelings.

Let your friends drive you to doctor appointments and treatments. Accept offers to bring food to supplement family meals, to take care of your children or pets, mow your lawn, or perform whatever tasks make life easier for you. Many times people want to help, but just don't know how. So tell them. (See *Tips for Caregivers*, p.53.) They will feel better, and so will you.

If you feel well enough to do the things you love—such as hobbies, visiting friends, working at your job, or volunteering—do them. Now might even be the time to indulge in a long-denied interest. Learn to knit, to play golf or bridge, sketch, practice yoga or Tai Chi—whatever makes you feel good without causing stress. When you are happy and relaxed, your body is stronger and better able to heal.

Humor. Laughter is therapeutic. It relaxes you and releases endorphins that can strengthen your immune system. Some cancer programs recommend watching comedies as part of their treatment programs. When I was undergoing treatments, I found myself drifting off to sleep at night watching *That Seventies Show*. Despite the annoying laugh track, it was therapy to my groggy mind.

I also had personal comedians in my friends and my husband, who was always finding ways to make me chuckle. One of my funniest memories after surgery is of Craig threatening to chase me around the house with a staple remover to take out my surgical staples. Then there was the friend who, upon learning of my brain surgery, instantly responded with perfect deadpan humor, "Did it help?" With friends and family like mine, who needs sit-coms?

Humor is just one way to activate the power of positive thinking. You can also stay positive by taking every opportunity to focus on the things, people, or places you love. I set up a special bulletin board decorated with mementoes and photos of people and places that made me feel happy. To this day, these are the first things I see when I wake up, and, along with kissing my husband goodbye and petting my sleeping dog at the foot of the bed, these images energize me with positive thoughts that set the tone for my day. I have posted other reminders around the house and my office, so I can smile with love and appreciation wherever I go. (See Chapter Five for more ideas on how to nurture a positive environment for healing.)

Fortified with hope, love, humor, and a positive attitude, you are ready to move forward and beat this thing!

Preparing for Therapy

You know your diagnosis and have a treatment plan. Now what do you do? How do you get ready for radiation and chemotherapy treatments? How do you deal with the possibility of losing your hair and the effects of nausea and fatigue? Preparation is the key.

Cancer veterans advised me to check first with the local American Cancer Society (ACS), which provides a variety of free and low-cost services to cancer patients. These include classes, free wig consultations and styling, head coverings, support groups, and other services for both men and women. You can locate your local chapter by logging on to the ACS website at *www.americancancersociety.org*, or by calling 1-800-227-2345 (1-866-228-4327 for TTY).

Depending on the type of drugs used, many people experience temporary hair loss during chemotherapy. I was one of the "lucky" ones, so my first move at the ACS was to make an appointment with a wig lady. She helped me understand what to look for in a wig and gave me two free ones, along with some head scarves and hats.

Although I appreciated the ACS wigs, they didn't feel like me, so I decided to go to a private salon that catered to the special needs of cancer patients. I paid about $200 for a fitting and a wig that brought lots of compliments. My insurance company covered most of the cost under "prosthetics." Your insurance company may do the same.

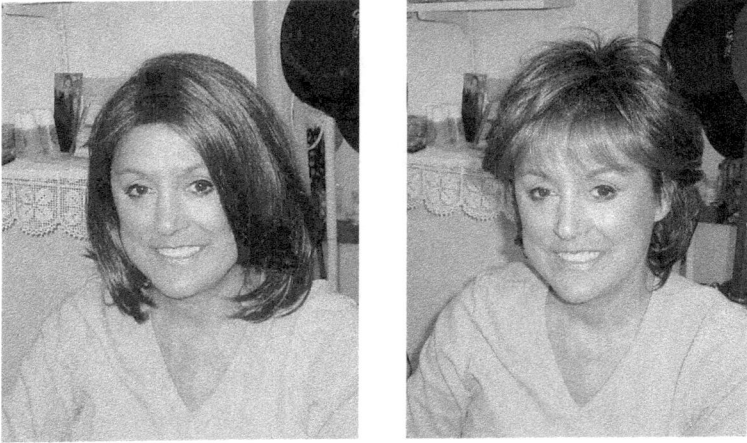

Fun with wigs – the long and short of it!

I highly recommend that women take care of this preparation sooner than later, since hair is often an important part of their identity. Men look stylish with a shaved head. Some women do, too, and I knew a few who shortcut the hair loss process, literally, by shaving their heads in advance of the "fall-out." They then decorated their shorn heads with a selection of attractive scarves and hats, having a little fun with the situation.

Males as well as females should stock up on hats to protect against heat loss through the head and against the sun's rays on newly exposed skin. Chilly nights may necessitate wearing the modern-day equivalent of a stocking cap to bed. I didn't like sleeping in a cap, so I used "Lulu," a floppy stuffed puppy that my husband gave me. Every night I perched my canine night stocking over the part of my bald head that protruded from the covers. Of course, by morning Lulu had usually abandoned her post for the floor or bottom of the bed. So much for (wo)man's best friend!

Getting to and from Treatments

You may need to have someone drive you to and from radiation and chemotherapy treatments. Anti-nausea drugs administered before chemotherapy infusions often cause drowsiness for several hours. The effects of radiation vary according to the area of the body being radiated. Ask your doctor in advance what to expect.

If you don't have a family member or friend to help with transportation, check with your place of worship, organizations you belong to, the ACS, your oncologist's office, or volunteer agencies in your area. Don't be afraid to ask others for help. Often friends and neighbors are glad to feel needed and anxious to know what they can do.

I found that the hours spent at chemotherapy sessions were a great opportunity to get to know my friends better. I was fortunate to have several willing and able volunteers. Another chemotherapy patient told me she turned her treatment sessions into mini-parties, inviting groups of friends to join her for snacks and board games.

Other suggestions to pass the time during long chemotherapy sessions include reading, chatting with other willing patients in the infusion room, doing a hobby, using your laptop, and watching TV. Or you may just want to sleep! Most infusion rooms have a variety of accommodations, both quiet and social, for patients' different needs. Check out the room in advance to get familiar with your options.

Dealing with Nausea

Nausea often accompanies chemotherapy and radiation treatments. Doctors can provide medications to help before, during, and afterwards. Most clinics include an anti-nausea medication with chemotherapy infusions. Ask your doctor what she provides and recommends.

A fellow chemotherapy patient suggested munching on light snacks to minimize nausea during infusions, which can last several hours. If you try this, make sure the food is light and bland. I found apples and cheese or peanut butter crackers worked best for me. Choose whatever appeals to you, and eat small portions slowly. I overdid it once and suffered the consequences later!

Stock up on "anti-nausea" foods before beginning treatments. You probably remember the foods mom used to give you when you had the flu as a child—saltine crackers, dry toast, bouillon, gelatin, clear juices—those bland comfort foods that you may have shunned as a nutrition-conscious adult. Although good nutrition is important, first and foremost, food must stay down! I heard about a patient who visited an acupuncturist before each chemotherapy session to help stem her nausea and increase her energy level afterwards.

Don't forget to keep yourself hydrated. Many chemotherapies cause thirst. Try sipping filtered water or clear juices both during and after therapy. Sucking on ice cubes or a frozen fruit Popsicle are other options to counteract nausea while hydrating your body.

Allow yourself to rest after treatments. Find a comfortable place free of distractions where you can take a nap. Remember, your body is undergoing a lot of stress during therapy, and you need to take care of yourself. This is one time when you shouldn't feel guilty about being "lazy." So indulge.

One friend with small children closed herself in her bedroom after she returned from therapy, relying on her husband to take care of the cooking and the kids. If a family member isn't an option, neighbors may be happy to help babysit. Take advantage of any resources.

Chemotherapy patients are often ultra-sensitive to odors. And, since the senses of smell and taste are intertwined, some odors may make you feel sick. I remember being quite nauseated by the smell of the chicken my husband loved to cook in our new rotisserie. "Rotisserie TV," he joked as he stared in anticipation at the chicken rotating behind the television-sized glass door. I failed to appreciate the humor and threatened to add him to the meal if he cooked another chicken! For months after my therapy ended, I couldn't even look at an advertisement for chicken! One chemotherapy veteran I know suggested avoiding contact with any foods you want to keep in your diet after therapy ends.

An Anti-Nausea Checklist

- ❑ **Get anti-nausea recommendations and prescriptions** before beginning treatment.

- ❑ **Eat bland foods,** such as saltine crackers, plain bagels, clear juices, fruit popsicles, and other non-spicy, non-greasy foods.

- ❑ **Avoid cooking meals.** If you don't have a family member to help, ask neighbors and friends to drop off ready-made meals, or check your eligibility for Meals on Wheels.

- ❑ **Eat small meals throughout the day,** rather than large ones.

- ❑ **Nibble on bland snacks** during infusions.

- ❑ **Avoid strong odors,** food or otherwise.

- ❑ **Rest** after treatments.

- ❑ **Eat what sounds good.** What you used to enjoy may no longer be appetizing.

- ❑ **Stay hydrated.**

"Chemo Brain"

Some cancer patients report experiencing a mental fog dubbed "chemo brain" both during and after treatment ends. This condition includes short-term memory loss and trouble focusing and multi-tasking. I initially assumed that these disorders were just a natural reaction to all the drugs being pumped into my body. However, I later learned that some cancer drugs may cause changes in brain activity that last even after therapy ends. In one study, scans of breast cancer patients who received chemotherapy versus those who did not showed changes in brain activity up to ten years after therapy ended.[7]

"Chemo brain" has only recently been formally recognized and studied. It primarily affects the parts of the brain that deal with memory, planning, putting thoughts into action, inhibition, and monitoring thought processes and behavior.[8] These are all critical functions that may influence one's ability to return to work or school and participate in social activities. I experienced some of these symptoms during treatment, but most of them disappeared or diminished over time. I still sometimes forget where I put my keys or cell phone, but I did that even before chemotherapy!

Managing the Symptoms of Chemo Brain

Don't despair, "chemo-brainers!" You can manage your symptoms by employing some simple techniques, many of which are helpful to anyone seeking to maintain optimal functioning, whether or not they've had chemotherapy.

First, keep a detailed daily planner, and write down details of appointments, medications, your "to-do" list, and locations of important documents or other resources that you might temporarily "forget." I did this regularly before getting sick, but found it to be more important than ever during and after treatment. Now my main concern is where I put my planner!

To manage this problem, I suggest trying to keep critical items in the same place all the time and returning them there immediately after use. I also find that verbalizing my intentions out loud helps to keep me on track. ("I put my glasses in my pocket," or, "Get pen and paper.") Fortunately, I work in a home office, without co-workers to accuse me of talking to myself!

Exercise, both physical and mental, is very important to maintaining brain health. Physical exercise increases blood flow to the brain as well as to the body, thereby improving mental alertness. Walking is known to be one of the best exercises for the body and mind. But don't forget to do your brain aerobics, as well. They range from activities such as reading or doing puzzles to participating in social events or taking an enrichment course of interest to you.

Maintaining your physical health is important to managing your mental health, as well. Get adequate rest and sleep—at least eight to nine hours, or more when undergoing therapy. Also, eat properly, especially vegetables. Studies show they can help maintain brain power.[9]

Finally, if you find that your symptoms are seriously interfering with your daily life, don't hesitate to tell your doctor. He may be able to refer you to a specialist for testing or therapy. Also, enlist the support of your family by letting them know what helps you deal with the symptoms, such as having more time to complete tasks. Their help and understanding may relieve some of the stress that can exacerbate chemo brain.

Working During Therapy

Journal entry six weeks into therapy:
Yesterday was a more stressful day. I went to a job interview, thinking I could pick up my life where I left off. I might have been pushing myself too hard, and I don't think it went very well. I'm fatigued and the medications affect my balance and ability to process thoughts.

If your job keeps you on track emotionally or financially, you may choose to continue working during treatment. If it brings you stress, however, consider taking a leave of absence or reducing your schedule for awhile. Remember, your body is already undergoing stress from therapy, so it is important to minimize stress from other sources. Your main job right now is to get and stay well.

When working during treatment, take breaks and relax whenever you can. Grab a quick nap at lunchtime, or get fresh air on a short walk. Research shows that catnaps as short as 15 minutes can "reboot" the brain and body.[10]

Therapy Preparation Checklist

❏ **Prepare for hair loss** by getting hats, scarves, and/or wigs.

❏ **Line up people to take you to and from treatments.**

❏ **Stock up on foods and medications that help with nausea.**

❏ **Stock up on fluids to stay well hydrated**: filtered water, juices, smoothies, teas, and other healthy fluids. (Avoid alcohol for now, as it may interact with your medications.)

❏ **Make a list of doctor, insurance, and emergency numbers** to post in your home and take with you wherever you go. Include a detailed list of any prescriptions and over-the-counter medications you are taking: names, strengths and dosages. Doctors and hospitals often ask for this information, which is also handy in emergencies. (You can use the tear-out form in the Appendix of this book.)

❏ **Set up a quiet, comfortable space** in your home where you can rest away from kitchen odors, children, or other disturbances.

❏ **Get a spiral notebook** (or set up your laptop computer) to keep a daily record of how you feel, the medications you are taking, your reactions to treatments, notes from doctor consultations, and any questions you have for your next doctor visit. This is a very handy tool for both you and your doctor. No two patients are the same, so this record will help monitor how your body reacts to treatments over time.

❏ **Get some good body lotion and sunscreen.** Treatments can dehydrate your skin and make it more sensitive to sunlight. Get products that are unscented and hypoallergenic, such as Cetaphil, to avoid irritating your skin.

❏ **Place photos, cards, sayings, and other inspirational items** by your bed and other locations you frequent, as reminders to keep your spirits up.

Tips for Caregivers and Others Who Want to Help

> *The gift of caring is the greatest gift of all.*

Asking for and accepting help is difficult for many people. Now is not the time, however, to prove your self-sufficiency. Your job is to heal, and people may want to help you. Let them. Many people feel uncomfortable with illness and don't know what to say or do. Help them help you by giving them these suggestions:

Flowers and plants. Sending flowers is nice, but they require care and may produce allergic reactions in those with a depressed immune system. Candy or fruit bouquets, balloons, or alternatives may be preferable. One cancer patient I know said the many arrangements of flowers in her house made her feel like she was at her own funeral! Personally, I liked the flowers, but preferred the green plants, because they lasted longer and needed less care. In fact, I still have a couple of them, and they continue to remind me of the kindness of those who sent them.

Cards and letters are always a good way to express how much you care. If the patient is technologically oriented, emails and online social networking sites like Facebook are also acceptable in contemporary society. They may not always substitute for the more personal touch of a card, but they can be a convenient way to maintain ongoing contact.

Those who are uncomfortable with what to say should just keep it simple and cheery. Avoid overly sympathetic thoughts that underscore the negative aspects of the situation. As one cancer survivor put it, "Words can just be inadequate. And, as we stumble and trip toward trying to say the right and true thing, we often reach for the nearest rotted-out cliché for support. Better to say nothing, and offer the gift of your presence, than to utter bankrupt bromides."[11]

Food and light treats are usually welcome, if not for the nauseous patient, perhaps for the family. Neighbors or church and social groups might want to set up a schedule for bringing by a meal or two each week. Make sure they are pre-cooked and only need a quick warm-up. It is also helpful to use disposable dishes that don't need to be washed and returned.

Gift certificates to local restaurants, movie theaters, video stores, or fast food places are great for both the patient and his family. If they are not used right away, they may be helpful later in the healing process.

Inspirational or humorous books that fit the recipient's interests and tastes may provide support and diversion.

Gift baskets of food, toiletries, or stationery and thank-you cards are useful, and easy to order from afar.

Offers to help with babysitting, laundry, shopping, mowing the lawn, or other light chores relieve burdens from the patient and family alike.

Staying in touch is very important. Continue to check in with the patient and family after the initial period of diagnosis and therapy. Don't assume they want to be left alone. They may feel isolated during this process and need to be reminded that people care. Interaction with friends and loved ones can be one of the best therapies.

A gathering of friends, impromptu or planned, can be a pleasant diversion for the patient. For guys, this might be an afternoon watching sports on TV. For women, perhaps you can plan an early evening "slumber party," where everyone shows up in pajamas with a good movie and popcorn. My wonderful neighbors organized one of these for me, and it was truly therapeutic. If the patient is mobile, hold the gathering at someone else's house, so the patient and family don't feel obligated to play host. Be sure to offer transportation, if needed.

Life Inside Out

Chapter 5:

Staying Strong to Get Well

The soul would have no rainbows if the eyes had no tears.
                                    - Native American saying

Journal entry two months into therapy:
Over the last few weeks, the effects of chemotherapy and radiation have begun to accumulate in my body and mind, and my bravado is beginning to succumb to the realization of how much my life has changed: Three years of therapy will take precedence over personal plans; my psyche has been forever altered by a new sense of vulnerability; I've begun to question my identity, as others now view me as "ill" and no longer the strong person I have always taken pride in being; my career is on hold as I make getting and staying well my primary job. So who am I now? A person with cancer? Do I have a new identity? Is there anything left of my former self?

Your body is under a great deal of stress right now, both physically and emotionally. It needs all the support it can get to deal with the disease and its treatments. As you progress through your therapy program, a relaxed and positive environment will help your body's defenses stay strong. So now is the time to arm your body with good physical and emotional care to fortify its disease-fighting resources.

Much has been written about the interplay of attitude, emotion, and health. Some believe that our minds have a material effect on what happens to us: that, at the molecular level, our thoughts attract positive or negative events into our lives. Gurus of positive thinking, such as Norman Vincent Peale, Wayne Dyer and Deepak Chopra, contend that thoughts can change our lives; that, if we embrace positive thoughts, good things will come to us.

We all know people who exemplify this concept—the sometimes annoyingly cheerful person who appears happy and positive, no matter what happens. Even bad things are turned around to something positive for these individuals, who never seem to let the world get them down. And the world often cooperates.

Then there are those who walk around with a black cloud of negativity hanging over their heads. For them the glass is always half empty, and they can only talk about how bad their lives are or will become. Not surprisingly, their negative expectations often materialize, and their lives seem to be a walking disaster full of "bad luck."

I choose to focus on the positive possibilities in my glass of life. Some say that approach has helped me succeed in my battle with illness. True or not, this attitude has at least helped me meet my challenges in a happier state.

When I was recovering from treatments, someone sent me a story that had been circulating on the Internet in various forms for years. It illustrates how we make attitudinal choices and is a good reminder of the importance of positive thinking.

> John is the kind of guy you love to hate. He is always in a good mood and always has something positive to say. When someone would ask him how he was doing, he would reply, "If I were any better, I would be twins!" He was a natural motivator. If someone was having a bad day, John was there telling them how to look on the positive side of the situation.

One day I went up and asked him, "I don't get it! You can't be a positive person all of the time. How do you do it?"

He replied, "Each morning I wake up and say to myself, you have two choices today. You can choose to be in a good mood or...you can choose to be in a bad mood. I choose to be in a good mood. Each time something bad happens, I can choose to be a victim or I can choose to learn from it. I choose to learn from it.

Every time someone comes to me complaining, I can choose to accept their complaining or I can point out the positive side of life. I choose the positive side of life."

"Yeah, right, it's not that easy," I protested.

"Yes, it is," he said. "Life is all about choices. When you cut away all the junk, every situation is a choice. You choose how you react to situations. You choose how people affect your mood. You choose to be in a good mood or bad mood. The bottom line: It's your choice how you live your life."

I reflected on what he said. Later we lost touch, but I often thought about him whenever I made a choice on how to react to life situations.

Several years later, I heard that he was involved in a serious accident, falling some 60 feet from a communications tower. After 18 hours of surgery and weeks of intensive care, he was released from the hospital with rods placed in his back.

I saw him about six months after the accident. When I asked him how he was, he replied, "If I were any better, I'd be twins... Wanna see my scars?" I declined to see his wounds, but I did ask him what had gone through his mind as the accident took place.

"The first thing that went through my mind was the well-being of my soon-to-be born daughter," he replied. "Then, as I lay on the ground, I remembered that I had two choices: I could choose to live or...I could choose to die. I chose to live."

"Weren't you scared? Did you lose consciousness?" I asked. He continued, "...the paramedics were great. They kept telling me I was going to be fine. But when they wheeled me into the ER and I saw the expressions on the faces of the doctors and nurses, I got really scared. In their eyes, I read, 'he's a dead man.' I knew I needed to take action."

"What did you do?" I asked. "Well, there was a big burly nurse shouting questions at me," said John. "She asked if I was allergic to anything. 'Yes,' I replied. The doctors and nurses stopped working as they waited for my reply. I took a deep breath and yelled, 'Gravity!'"

"Over their laughter, I told them, 'I am choosing to live. Operate on me as if I am alive, not dead.'" He lived, thanks to the skill of his doctors, but also because of his amazing attitude... I learned from him that every day we have the choice to live fully. Attitude, after all, is everything.

The Healing Attitude

Attitude is a powerful tool for getting through life's challenges, even a deadly disease. Our attitude not only affects our emotional well-being, but studies show it can make a difference in our physical health, as well. How does this work? Our bodies are made up of very small units of energy called atoms. Within the last century or so, scientists have recognized an even smaller unit of energy in our bodies, called quanta. Quanta are made up of invisible vibrations waiting to take physical form as energy-producing particles of matter.

These particles form the basis of everything we are—thoughts, emotions, cells, and organs, any visible or invisible part of ourselves. Our nervous system can sense the faint vibrations of the quanta, and signals from the quanta can cause instantaneous changes in the physical body. Hence, when our thoughts are at a negative energy level, our bodies respond at that same level, and vice versa.[12]

What thoughts can produce low energy and weaken us? Thoughts of anger, hatred, fear, shame, worry, and criticism. On the other hand, positive thoughts and feelings of love and kindness can strengthen our immune systems by increasing our serotonin levels. When you consider that every year 98% of our body's cells are replaced, imagine the implications the mind-body connection has for our long-term health!

Staying Positive

How do you stay positive when you feel like a glowing pincushion and most of the time can't decide whether you want to sleep, vomit, or cry? Pretty unrealistic, you say? Nothing about this process is easy, but positive thinking techniques are, at the very least, enjoyable. And that's the idea.

Start with small, easy steps. Surround yourself with happy reminders of people, places, and things that make you smile. Leave out anything that will make you nostalgic or sad. My bedroom, office and refrigerator are decorated with photos of people and places I love, thoughtful cards from well-wishers, humorous cartoons, and inspirational sayings. My décor may not qualify for a feature in *House Beautiful Magazine*, but it is a daily reminder to smile and be grateful for the gifts in my life.

Another approach to keeping your spirits up is to write a "Love List" of all the things that nourish your soul—from simple, everyday pleasures like sweatpants and your favorite slippers, to special treats like sitting by a mountain stream or riding in a car with the top down. Then put the list someplace where you will see it, add to it, and focus on its content with gratitude. The positivism that this list generates may become a magnet, attracting healing and good things into your life. As Deepak Chopra says, "If you have happy thoughts, then you make happy molecules." You can also use the list to neutralize things that make you feel bad, like waiting for MRI results or paying bills.

Another way to imprint positive thoughts on your mind is to start and end each day by counting your blessings, which are always there, no matter how bad things may seem. Think about the people you love and who love you: your caregivers, professional and personal, your family, friends, and nature's amazing tableau outside your window. Be grateful for all the past, present, and future beauty of life.

Whether or not you are spiritual, you may find support in prayer or other personal verbalizations of your hopes and concerns. Words, whether said aloud or in your head, articulate the reality you want for yourself and can change your mood. Singing them enhances the process. Whenever I'm feeling a bit down, I sing a cheerful song in my head (sometimes out loud, if no one's listening) that reflects my hope for the day. My usual choice is "Oh, What a Beautiful Morning," from the musical Oklahoma. Find something catchy that is upbeat and has a positive meaning for you personally. Then get in the shower and belt it out!

If you prefer to have someone else do the singing, try awakening to your favorite music on the radio or iPod. You could even do a silly dance to get your blood circulating and further set the upbeat mood of the day. Or not. I'm not that quick on my feet when I first wake up!

While emphasizing the positive, it is also important to minimize the negative. The daily news can be very depressing, so I recommend limiting negative TV shows and ending each day with a comedy or something uplifting. I went to sleep each night listening to the sound of the surf I love so much, provided by a machine that can also mimic rain, wind, or other soothing sounds to ease me into slumber and into the next day on a positive note.

Stress and Dis-ease

Stress, like gravity, is a natural and necessary part of our lives. It is a countervailing force that pushes us to accomplish life's everyday tasks and provides the body's natural "fight or flight" response to danger. It is a positive factor when experienced in limited amounts.

Stress also has a darker side. This is the side we usually associate with feeling overwhelmed by responsibilities or with experiencing affronts to our sense of self, such as being insulted or cut off in traffic. Less recognized is the stress that results from feeling powerless, as when we're in an unfulfilling job, a bad relationship, or when we are ill and unable to function normally. A life-threatening illness is a high stressor for everyone associated with it, from the patient and family to friends and caregivers.

Whether positive or negative, stress in large or persistent doses can disrupt our body's natural defenses and affect its ability to heal. The stress hormones noradrenalin and cortisol inhibit the body's immune response to abnormal cells by initiating an inflammation process that may be instrumental in the development and spread of cancer cells. With its disease-fighting mechanisms weakened, the body becomes more susceptible to illness. Recent research has even revealed a connection between stress and some autoimmune diseases.[13] Managing stress is critical to getting and staying well.

> *Free from desire, you realize the mystery. When you are content to be simply yourself, and don't compare or compete, everybody will respect you.*
> *-Tao Te Ching*

Given what I now know about the physiological effects of stress, I can't help wondering about the role it might have played in allowing cancer to take hold in my body. Perhaps the tumor would have emerged at some point anyway, but did I open the gate and welcome it in by allowing stress to weaken my body's natural defense system?

In the months before cancer reared its ugly head, I was feeling great stress in my professional life. It was affecting my personal relationships and lifestyle, which, in turn, increased my level of anxiety. I wasn't eating properly, relying on comfort foods and diet drinks to soothe my emotions. My husband complained that I was leaving half-used cans of soda scattered around the house, and lights on everywhere I went (one of his pet peeves). Was that an early warning of the growth swelling in my head, or signs of the stress that was making me vulnerable? I believe it was both.

Depression

After my diagnosis, I had to straddle the negative and positive sides of stress. My new jobless lifestyle of doctor appointments, napping, and therapies left me without the structure that had previously both sustained and stressed me. I was not able to work full-time after cancer was discovered. During the time when I felt sickest, not having to work was a blessing, because I had fewer demands in my life. However, as I became more able to function normally, I often felt the "floating effect" of not having enough pressure to propel myself forward. I had to learn simultaneously to relax and to create a daily structure of my own. This led to minor bouts of depression, which is not uncommon in cancer patients or others dealing with life-altering diseases.

It is understandable to feel depressed when you have a serious illness. This is a natural reaction and nothing to be embarrassed about. Symptoms often include feeling sad, being unmotivated, and using sleep as an escape. These could also be very normal reactions to the illness or medications. Nevertheless, if you experience these symptoms excessively or for a prolonged period of time, you should talk to your doctor, who may be able to help by adjusting your medications or prescribing an anti-depressant.

Keep in mind that it is not just the patient who risks depression. Often the primary caregiver and family members are subject to similar stresses and may need to seek help as well. There is no shame in feeling depressed. What is important is to recognize and do something about it. Denial can just lead to more stress.

Everyday Ways To Elevate Your Mood

Apart from medical solutions, there are simple, everyday ways to elevate your mood. Engage in regular, moderate exercise, such as walking, swimming, yoga, Tai Chi, or other forms of activities suitable for your condition and approved by your physician. Outdoor exercise may be especially helpful, because it provides the healthy effects of fresh air and Vitamin D from sunshine.

Participate in social activities, such as visits with friends, cultural or sporting events, travel, or anything that allows you to be among other people in an enjoyable and supportive environment. Since your immune system is weakened by chemotherapy and other treatments, ask your doctor if you should avoid crowds, air travel, or other potential exposures to illness. For these situations, my primary care physician recommended taking a vitamin supplement such as Airborne and putting a dab of anti-bacterial ointment in each nostril prior to exposure, to be blown out afterwards.

Reducing Stress

Journal entry four months into therapy:
Life is art. Perhaps that is why it did my soul so much good to go to art class again last night. I was met with hugs and beautiful people, and creative works. Therapy.

Western medicine has only recently emphasized the mind-body connection, so you may have to look east for many stress-reducing therapies. Eastern medicine has a history of holistic health practices such as Yoga, acupuncture, Tai Chi, aromatherapy, and meditation, all of which are meant to promote relaxation and total body wellness. A good blend of Western and Eastern therapies may be the best approach to maintaining your health during treatment.

Having fun is another way to reduce stress. When you participate in an enjoyable activity, your body gets a "natural high" from the release of endorphins. Endorphins are the neurotransmitters in the brain responsible for reducing our perception of pain. They also act to reduce stress and enhance the body's immune response.[14]

This is particularly true with creative endeavors. Now is an opportunity to indulge yourself in something enjoyable that you might not ordinarily do. Below are some creative activities believed to relieve stress and promote healing.

Music has a long history of being linked to healing. Its vibrations facilitate the mind-body-spirit connection. Sound has measurable effects on the physical body, influencing energy flow and balancing brain waves. The singing voice, for example, with its use of breath, vibration, and emotion, can affect the body and mind more efficiently than any other form of sound. So whip out your favorite CDs or iPod and sing along! Soothing music may be especially relaxing during infusion sessions.

Writing. Journaling is an effective and easy way to release and understand your feelings as you progress through cancer. Writing has always been my passion, so it was relaxing and cathartic for me to write down my feelings and discoveries in the daily journal that formed the basis for this book. I particularly enjoy writing poetry, some of which is featured in this book.

You don't have to be a writer to benefit from journaling. All it takes is a blank piece of paper, a pen or pencil (Try crayons or colored pencils for a creative change), or, if you prefer, a computer keyboard. No one will be grading you, so just write whatever comes to your mind, without censoring or worrying about grammar. You can always erase or throw it away when you're done. You may find, however, that keeping it and referring back to previous thoughts gives you a sense of progress and perspective.

If you have problems getting words out, try keeping your hands moving without stopping, even if the words don't make sense. Once you get going, you might be amazed at what appears. Try playing background music to spur you on.

> *Art brushes away from the soul the dust of everyday life.*
> *–Pablo Picasso*

Painting. Creating visual art through painting or drawing is another recognized healing therapy. By connecting to your own creativity, you gain a sense of empowerment when you may feel out of control in every other sense. It also actively transports you from your left-brain world of worry and stress to the right-brain world of play and being in the moment. You don't have to take lessons to benefit from creating art. Think back to the days when scribbling a picture with crayons was a delight. Then get out your crayons or brushes and fill the paper with color, shapes, and fun!

Crafts. Crafts are another way to exercise your creativity. Try knitting, model building, origami, sewing, needlepoint, woodworking, or anything else that involves working with the right side of the brain, the side responsible for creativity. The important thing is to relax and enjoy.

Scents. Most people are buoyed by pleasant fragrances, and some believe that the sense of smell can influence emotional and physical health. The ancient practice of aromatherapy, which uses fragrant oils as therapy for a variety of ills, is increasingly recognized for its healing benefits. Aromatherapy purports, for example, that lavender scents aid relaxation and lemon elevates mood. The science of these claims is disputed by some, but most people agree that certain scents make them feel good. For me it's the scent of a rose, a vanilla candle, or the freshly-ironed smell of a warm spring morning.

Because my tumor and surgery were in my head, my sense of smell was temporarily affected. The tumor had pressed against an olfactory nerve, resulting in over sensitivity to odors, particularly unpleasant ones. When I was released from the hospital after surgery, I spent two hours in the scented candle section of a department store with my cousin Marcie, inhaling the sweet, soothing aromas to erase and replace odiferous memories. It was perfect therapy!

What fragrances make you feel good? Surround yourself with the scents you enjoy. Strategically placed candles, sachets, sprays (Try a spray of lavender on your pillow.), or bouquets of flowers can be easy ways to boost your mood and help you relax as you get through treatments and embark on your path to wellness.

The Power of Laughter

> *Find joy in everyday things—appreciate, laugh, en-joy. Be in joy.*
> *- Sark*

The connection between laughter and healing has been well documented. Laughter triggers the release of endorphins, the body's natural pain killers. It also encourages immune-building reactions in the body.

My brain surgery was perfect fodder for good-natured jokes, which kept me laughing throughout an otherwise difficult time. Besides the expected references to having a hole in my head, my family, friends, and I had great fun when I got fitted for a wig. My brother touched up my wig photo with a mustache, and some old friends expressed their solidarity and senses of humor by greeting me at an airport terminal in a psychedelic array of colorful wigs. I kept photos of the fun on my refrigerator to re-live the humor every day.

Support

Seek support systems that allow you to relax and leave daily chores behind. Let someone else cook, or use pre-packaged foods. Forget about having a clean house if you have no one to help with that. An international organization, Cleaning for a Reason, provides free house cleaning once a month up to four months for patients undergoing chemotherapy. It has participating maid services in all 50 states and Canada. Check its website at *www.cleaningforareason.org* for information and to apply.

Pets and Other Furry Comforts

Health experts have long recognized the positive effects of pets, which are often used in therapy programs at hospitals and care facilities. Stroking a beloved cat or having a dog greet you with a wagging tail is instant therapy. Research has shown that 15-30 minutes with a pet are enough to significantly lower the stress hormone cortisol and raise production of serotonin, a chemical associated with feelings of well-being.[15] Even watching goldfish swim can make a person feel less stressed.[16] Have you ever noticed how many doctor offices have aquariums?

If you don't already have a dog or a cat, this may not be the best time to break one in. Ask your physician or hospital about the availability of a local pet therapy program. Or, if you are mobile, perhaps you could visit pet shops or volunteer at a local animal daycare or shelter. (Note: Since you may be emotionally vulnerable, be wary of getting attached to a shelter animal that might be euthanized.)

The next best thing may be a furry substitute, such as a stuffed animal. At the risk of sounding sexist, I'll suggest that women may appreciate this option more than guys. But maybe not; there are fun stuffed animals that may appeal to both sexes, and anyone can find comfort in something to hug. They have the added benefit of making no demands for food or walks!

Relaxation

Indulge yourself. Take naps whenever you feel like it, without guilt. This is an important part of your therapy. You might also want to try relaxation therapies such as massages, facials, acupressure, acupuncture, Reiki (therapeutic movement of body heat), or just a Jacuzzi or warm bath. Talk to your doctor before engaging in any special treatments, to see if she can recommend practitioners who have experience working with the unique needs of cancer patients.

Massage

Massage can be a wonderful therapy both during and after cancer treatments. Performed by a professional trained in working with cancer patients, massage can help relieve discomfort and stress by increasing circulation and releasing endorphins, the body's natural painkillers. Even foot massages can be very helpful in promoting a healing environment in your body. Some cancer treatment facilities offer these free or at low cost.

Simply taking the time to relax in the care of a massage therapist can provide a restorative and healing experience. Although most medical professionals acknowledge the benefits of gentle massage in supplementing cancer treatments, you should check with your physician beforehand. Deep pressure may be inadvisable after certain medical treatments. The massage therapist can work in concert with your doctor to coordinate the timing and intensity of massage therapy with your cancer treatments.

Journal entry five months into therapy:
Drink in each day: sip and savor each moment. Find the joy in now. Every day is a gift, to be lovingly unwrapped with wonder and awe, and received with gratitude and joy.

Appreciating the Moment

One of the first books recommended to me during my illness was *The Power of Now*, by Eckhart Tolle. I found its central point--to appreciate each moment, the *now* of life--to be particularly relevant. After all, that's what life really is. The past is gone and the future not yet here. So we can only experience the moment, the now.

Focusing on the now is a simple way of meditating and appreciating life. Once I started practicing awareness of the moment, I found myself stopping to admire the moon on a starry night, the glow of white lights on snowy bushes, a passing child's smile, a playful squirrel on the backyard fence, or just the design of shadows on a wall. There is nothing like the threat of life denied to enhance one's enjoyment of each small moment that it offers. So much gets lost in the hustle and hurry of the "to-do-list" life. Gratitude for each moment, each sunrise and sunset, helps promote balance and put things in perspective. This concept is also extolled in my favorite poem from the Sanskrit, which I memorized in my youth and never truly understood until recently:

Look to this Day!
For it is Life, the Very Life of Life.
In its brief course lie all the verities
and realities of your existence.
The Bliss of Growth,
The Glory of Action,
The Splendor of Beauty;
For Yesterday is but a Dream,
And To-morrow is only a Vision:
But To-day well-lived makes every
Yesterday a Dream of Happiness,
And Every To-morrow a Vision of Hope.
Look well, therefore, to this Day!
Such is the Salutation of the Dawn.

Author unknown. From the Sanskrit, "The Salutation of the Dawn."

Taking Charge

Basically, we are our own best doctors. Although we certainly need the knowledge, technologies, and services of medical experts, we know ourselves best and should use that knowledge to help our doctors help us. As one lovely and feisty lady advised me after hearing about my diagnosis, "You must take charge." During her own successful battle with cancer more than 25 years earlier, she had discovered that doctors can't know everything, so we must be advocates for our own health. I owe a debt of gratitude to former Colorado First Lady Dottie Lamm for that valuable advice. To the occasional vexation of my doctors, her counsel stood me in good stead during my cancer experience.

Experts say that patients who participate in their own healing process are less likely to feel helpless and vulnerable, which improves their emotional well-being. Taking charge can mean anything from becoming well informed about your challenge and its potential remedies, to asking questions and recording the details of your responses to medical treatment.

For me it meant researching everything I could find related to wellness. I read numerous books on physical and emotional well-being; I checked out therapies on the Internet; and I consulted a variety of wellness practitioners, from naturopaths and nutritionists to chiropractors and physician specialists. One friend said her nurse recommended only consulting websites with the extensions "edu" or "org," because their information is more likely to be authoritative and backed by research.

Taking charge also means communicating your needs and desires clearly to your healthcare providers. It is important to let your doctors know what is going on with your body as you experience it from the inside. Keeping them informed about any pains, discomforts, or unexplained symptoms will help them diagnose and determine the best steps to take in your therapy. Doctors are physicians, not psychics, so they need your help.

Perhaps most important of all, taking charge means standing up for yourself when you feel that you should be doing something different from what your doctor recommends. As knowledgeable as doctors are, they don't know your body in the same way you do. Remember, they have many bodies to take care of, and you have only one.

I had an occasion to exercise Dottie's advice when I felt one of my chemotherapies might be causing hearing loss. I did some online research on the suspected drug and consulted with my ear doctor. He confirmed that my increased hearing loss could, in fact, be a side-effect of that drug. He shared this information with my oncologist, who, after checking into the situation, took me off the suspicious drug. Not only had I taken charge of my own health, but my doctors had listened and responded—proof, in my mind, that we were a team in the healing game.

Daily Rituals

Rituals and routines provide a sense of continuity and comfort that can be especially reassuring in uncertain times. The mindless repetition of actions can also serve as a form of meditation.

Even during my worst times, I made a point of observing daily rituals, especially upon rising. The drugs I was taking made it hard to wake up, so the rituals helped me merge softly into the day. If you are still working, job responsibilities may provide the rituals you need. However, many people have to stop or cut back on work during cancer treatments, which can disrupt their daily structure and be disorienting. If that is your situation, you may have to create new rituals of your own design.

My daily rituals included prayers, checking email, watering plants, and doing yoga exercises to get the blood flowing in my veins. Newly jobless friends said it helped them to go to their computers first thing in the morning as if they were going to the office. Others found a brisk early morning would set their heads on straight for the day.

Looking Forward and Having Fun

> *Some say life is short. I say life is TALL—Grab a straw!*
> *— Sark*

Another structural aid, like rituals, is to have something to look forward to and plan for, such as a special trip, an outing, or the completion of an enjoyable project. Most doctors I know encourage patients to participate in fun activities and will schedule treatments around them when possible. They recognize the role of fun in aiding healing.

There are organizations that arrange outings and activities for seriously ill patients, sometimes providing financial support as well. Perhaps the best known is the Make a Wish Foundation *www.wish.org*. However, local communities often have organizations, as well. Ask your doctor or local Cancer Society for resources in your community. Yes, it's important to take it easy, but don't stop living in the process!

The Power of Prayer

I'm not into organized religion, but I do believe in a universal spirit of love and the power of prayer. I have personally experienced it. When I was under anesthesia during my emergency operation, a friend organized a prayer circle for me many miles away. I feel sure its healing energy played a role in helping me come out of the operation successfully. Even the surgeon was amazed at my quick recovery. Perhaps the energy of that prayer circle had reached across the miles to that operating room. Scientific research indicates the existence of an energy field that can be impacted by positive or negative energy generated by oneself or those around us.[17]

No matter what your religious or spiritual beliefs are, I strongly recommend that you spend some portion of each day in prayer or "innerspeak," the internal dialogue we all have with ourselves. By expressing and summoning the power to achieve your desires, you are putting your needs into the universe, and there is power in your words.

Because of my experience directing an international exchange program, I was the fortunate recipient of many different kinds of prayers—from Hindu rituals and Muslim blessings to Catholic masses and non-denominational good wishes in many sizes and shapes. A Hindu friend in India performed prayer ceremonies for me during each of my treatments; Muslim friends from Iraq and Egypt prayed to Allah for my health; a decorated gourd from a Christian friend in Ghana, inscribed with symbols that said in his native Twi the words "Gye Nyame," ("Accept the omnipotence of God") provided a daily reminder of the greater power available to help me make it through this dark time. Christian, Jewish, agnostic and even atheist friends sent prayers and positive thoughts. I know these made a difference, if in no other way than through a demonstration of caring that buoyed my heart. In addition, personally tapping into the power of prayer allowed me to find strength and light within myself.

I was amused by my friend Debbie, who, after being diagnosed with breast cancer, joked that so many people offered to pray for her that she imagined God was feeling "positively harassed," to the point of saying, "Okay, fine, I'll cure this woman! Get off my back already!" She then urged her supporters to keep up the pressure, just in case.

There's strength in numbers, and in positive thoughts, prayers or not. Prayer, meditation, and faith in some kind of higher power can provide comfort and support to get you through the worst of times. Much has been written about the impact of faith in helping people survive times of crisis. In fact, there are those who purport that faith in a higher power of some kind is a determining factor in overcoming seemingly impossible odds.

Daily Reminders for Staying Strong During Treatment

- **Be kind to yourself.** Rest when needed and pamper yourself.
- **Surround yourself with inspiration**—people, sayings, photos and mementoes that make you smile.
- **Laugh frequently.**
- **Be in the moment:** Notice the colors of the day and think how lucky you are to be here to enjoy them.
- **Take charge of your own health.** Monitor your reactions to therapies and communicate your observations and questions to your doctors.
- **Establish daily rituals.**
- **Make plans for the future.**
- **Engage in prayer, meditation, or some form of positive inner-speak every day.**
- **Keep a journal** of your feelings.
- **Get fresh air and moderate exercise** as much as possible.
- **Eat nutritiously.** (See Chapter Six)
- **Spend time with friends and family.**
- **Participate in events and activities** as much as possible.

Chapter 6:

A New Beginning:
Staying Healthy After Treatment Ends

Journal entry at the end of treatment:
They say you can only be sure of two things in life—death and taxes—and I just scored significant victories over both. Today our accountant informed us that we don't owe any additional taxes; and last week I successfully completed my three-year cancer treatment program and attended the Annual Survivor's Party. Life is good!

I continue to fight the effects of the Shingles virus that damaged the cornea of my right eye. I may never see normally out of that eye again. But I remind myself that this is a small price to pay for still being present on this wonderful earth. Nothing is forever, but I am just grateful for the now. Yes, life is good!

Moving On

It's the end of your treatment program. Perhaps your hair is growing back, your blood count is returning to normal, and you're growing stronger. You're ready to move on. You have done your tour of duty. You have paid your dues. All the trite phrases apply: Close this chapter! Shut the door! GET ON WITH IT!

So what is *it?* Life as it once was is no more. You're a different person now, having viewed life from the inside out. A scar of vulnerability is forever etched on your soul. You know, really know, that there are no guarantees. And, if you start to forget, there are always those periodic checkups to remind you!

No matter how far you travel, your cancer experience always remains visible in the distance. You are ever aware of where you came from, reminded by the mud on your feet and the sweat on your brow. You may have changed physically, mentally, and emotionally from the person you were "BC." But, although the path may still be challenging, you have crossed a significant border back into the Land of Tomorrow. You want to make sure cancer never slows your journey again—or, worse yet, ends it.

When I was able to raise my sites from the myopia of therapies and doctor appointments, I was ready to view my world from a more holistic perspective again. Most of all, I was ready to rebuild my health and stay that way. So I dove into reading and researching the relationship between a healthy lifestyle and cancer prevention.

This chapter contains a summary of the information I found most promising for building and maintaining an immune system strong enough to stand up against a potential recurrence of cancer. The content is based primarily on the sources cited at the end of the book. For more in-depth information on any of the following topics, I recommend reading the sources themselves.

Why Cancer?

Being analytical, I first wanted to know why I got cancer. If I could understand why, perhaps I could avoid taking that path again. Was it something I ate, drank, inhaled, or absorbed? Could I blame cell phones, computers, TVs, and the many other electromagnetic fields (EMFs) in contemporary life? How about the Polyvinylchloride (PVC) in second-hand smoke and in the walls and pipes of our mountain chalet? Both of these have been identified as possible causes of brain cancer.

If these carcinogens were the villains, why did I succumb to their toxins when others didn't? Why do some hi-risk women get breast cancer when others don't? Or some men with high PSA counts get prostate cancer when others don't? And why do some life-time smokers get lung cancer, when others continue smoking into old age and remain untouched? Is it genes? lifestyle? fate? or just *"Sh*t happens!"*?

As I researched these questions, I discovered that the answer is probably all of the above. Cancer, I learned, is not as much a disease as a condition. It is the combination of a tendency, perhaps a genetic predisposition, and a triggering event. We all have stray cells roaming our bodies that are capable of initiating cancer, but they are normally contained and destroyed by our immune system.[18] Unfortunately, our immune system occasionally loses the battle and the cancer cells go wild, feeding on damaged areas of the body to multiply and disrupt normal functioning.

Given the intelligence and tenacity of our immune system, it's amazing that disease-causing intruders ever get past the many barriers our bodies have in place. But I have learned that we often ally with the invaders by mistreating and neglecting our health. We take our bodies for granted, even after they plead for attention through aches, pains, or illness. We usually respond with mere appeasements, such as medications or medical procedures. And once the symptoms of disease are relieved, we go on our merry way, without even a cursory thanks to our hard-working immune system. Worse yet, we often resume the practices that welcomed disease in the first place!

What Helps?

After reading Dr. David Servan-Schreiber's informative book *Anti-Cancer*, I have a new appreciation for the impact of daily life choices on our health. Although I have always recognized the importance of a healthy lifestyle, the information in his book has raised my awareness of the many factors that play a role in preventing illness and keeping our bodies strong—from diet, sleep, and exercise to the less commonly emphasized influences of environment, attitude, and even breathing. The author illustrates the relationship between our most basic activities and the maintenance of a healthy, cancer-free life.

It took a recurrence of the same kind of cancer that I had, GBM, to spur Dr. Servan-Shreiber to change his lifestyle and write his book. Diana Dyer, in her excellent book on nutrition, *A Dietitian's Cancer Story*, tells how she experienced three bouts of cancer before she finally woke up and took her own advice on proper nutrition. I don't want to wait as long as these two authors did to make healthy choices in my life. I hope the information in this next chapter will encourage others to act now, too, whether or not they have ever had cancer.

This chapter provides an overview of basic concepts for maintaining a strong defense against cancer and other illnesses. As a layperson, I present these concepts in general terms. For more in-depth information, I recommend reading the above-mentioned books or others listed in the Appendix of this book. I also recommend re-visiting Chapter Five, as many of its suggestions for getting through treatment, such as minimizing stress and staying positive, are equally valid for maintaining health after treatment ends.

These are the basic premises on which I base the recommendations in this chapter:

- We all have the potential for cancer in our bodies.
- Our bodies have natural mechanisms for fighting cancer and other diseases.
- We have the power to strengthen or weaken our body's natural disease-fighting mechanisms through our actions.
- Those actions include our approaches to diet, exercise, lifestyle, and stress reduction.

What is Cancer?

To defend myself from a recurrence of cancer, I realized that I must understand my enemy. So I submitted myself to a crash course in cancer biology by studying the explanations in my resources. I learned that cancer usually initiates from rogue cells that have mutated due to a genetic miscue or tissue damage from injury or infection.[19] The inflammatory response of the body to such disturbances can cause a predisposition for cancer development, particularly when the response is chronic.

Often the tissue most vulnerable to cancer has been damaged earlier in life or over time—such as lungs clogged by longtime smoking or asbestos exposure; stomach, throat, or intestines inflamed by chronic digestive problems; skin damaged by repeated overexposure to the sun; everyday sores that never heal; or even scarring from an old wound. (I can't help but wonder about that blow to my head when I fell out of a tree as a child and broke my back.)

Inflammation is the body's natural response to injury or infection. It is most commonly visible around cuts, insect bites, and even pimples. When the body's immune system reacts to an irritated or damaged area, it sends in troops of white and red blood cells for a self-limiting period of time. The white blood cells that are the First Responders are backed up by a crew of red blood cells from capillaries, to provide sustenance and waste disposal to the affected area. When the wound is healed, these immune cells usually stand down.

However, in the case of a cancerous tumor, immune cells refuse to halt operations. Cancer cells require a quickly replenished supply of red blood cells to keep up their rapid growth. So they produce a chemical substance called angiogenin to attract more immune cells, a process called angiogenesis. Much chemotherapy is designed to prevent the formation of new capillaries, thereby cutting off cancer's supply line. Dr. Servan-Schreiber describes the process thus:

> ...cancer is a tricky demon and its cells don't respond normally to the body's defenses. They find ways ...to continue to grow and spread their poison in other locations in the body, thus shutting down normal body functions in the areas they invade.
>
> Angiogenesis, or neovascularization, involves the proliferation of new blood vessels. The process transforms a small, usually harmless cluster of abnormal cells (known as an in situ tumor) into a large mass that can spread to other organs. Intervention (dietary, chemotherapy, radiation, etc.) that interferes with the making of new blood vessels can prevent the growth of tumors, maintaining them in a dormant state. Under some circumstances, it may even make an existing tumor regress.[20]

The basic message I draw from this explanation is that inflammation can be food to cancer. So when we do things that continually irritate and, thus, inflame and damage our tissues, we could be encouraging mutant cancer cells to develop and spread.

The pharmaceutical world offers scores of products to quell inflammation, ranging from over-the-counter remedies to prescription drugs. I have learned that there are also many non-medicinal ways to reduce or eliminate cancer's inflammatory prey and strengthen the body's natural ability to defend itself.

First and foremost, we can reduce or eliminate any elective practices that produce harmful inflammation in our bodies—i.e., quit smoking, change our diets, protect our skin from over-exposure to sun, avoid environmental toxins, etc. These are risk factors we can control.

I was amazed to learn that genetic defects over which we have no control are responsible for only about 15 percent of all cancer deaths. [21] This indicates that up to 85 percent of all cancer mortalities may result from risk factors over which we do have control, giving us the personal power to prevent most cancer deaths. Our everyday choices in diet, activities, and even thoughts can influence our immune system and its ability to keep cancerous inflammation in check.

Immune Cells Are Our Friends

Our blood contains microscopic navies of immune cells that form our body's personal Department of Defense. We can fortify or weaken these protectors by how we treat our bodies. Some foods and nutrients, for example, are said to naturally inhibit angiogenesis and reduce harmful inflammation. These include certain edible mushrooms, green teas, spices, and herbs.[22]

On the other hand, there are some foods and nutrients that promote angiogenesis, such as an excess of Omega 6 oils not balanced properly with the good effects of Omega 3s.[23] This excess may promote inflammation, so it is important to proceed cautiously with self-medication through natural remedies.

I highly recommend consulting professional nutritionists or pharmacologists trained in the interactions of natural supplements and drugs before beginning any supplemental regimen. This is especially critical for those still undergoing chemotherapy. Let your doctor know about any nutritional supplements you take. Some doctors remain skeptical of supplements, so the more you arm yourself with information about them from credible sources, the better.

Nutrition: Food plays a major role in our immune capabilities, both negative and positive. Certain foods, such as refined sugars, drive up inflammatory insulin in our blood, and other foods, such as cauliflower and broccoli, are said to have properties capable of preventing precancerous cells from developing into malignant tumors. Because we are constantly feeding our bodies, Servan-Schreiber says, "Cancer is like diabetes. You must look after it every day."[24]

There are many good books on nutrition, but I found two to be especially relevant to cancer prevention: *A Dietitian's Cancer Story*, by Diana Dyer, and *How to Prevent and Treat Cancer with Natural Medicine*, by Dr. Michael Murray. An encyclopedic reference on nutrition may also be helpful as a guide. I like *Natural Detoxification* by Jacqueline Krohn, MD, and Frances Taylor, MA, but there are many other good resources available and easily found in most natural food stores. In addition, The American Cancer Society has a free booklet on eating hints during treatment, which you may also find at your oncologist's office. Or you can refer to the National Cancer Institute's website at *www.5aday.gov.*

It's easy to get overloaded with technical information on nutrition, and many resources often say the same things in different ways. So, after much research, I have boiled down the nutritional stew to a summary of basic points:

Healthy Eating 101

Eat a diet rich in fruits and vegetables, especially fresh, organic ones when you can. Consume a *minimum* of five servings, or 3-1/2 cups, a day (equivalent to one cup orange juice, one medium apple, a small green salad and one-half cup cooked green beans or peas). More is even better. Try to get at least one serving with each meal and two for between-meal snacks. Think color, as in broccoli, kale, sweet potatoes, carrots, plums, tomatoes, blueberries, and strawberries. The deeper the color, the more antioxidant properties.

The phytochemicals in vegetables and fruits that help protect them from decay contain antioxidant properties that also help us when we consume them. Anti-oxidants inhibit free radicals, the highly reactive chemicals that damage cells and make us more vulnerable to cancer. Spinach, tomatoes, grapefruit, and carrots contain high levels of an important immunity boosting agent called Glutathione. This powerful antioxidant is most effective when absorbed from foods, rather than supplements. Rich supplies can also be found in walnuts, avocados, and fresh fruits.

Fresh or frozen produce is best, as canning destroys most cancer-fighting chemicals.

When cooking vegetables, lightly steam or stir-fry them in olive oil to retain the most nutrients and phytochemicals. Don't overcook; they should retain their crispness and color.

Drink at least 6-8 glasses (48-64 oz.) of water every day. It's not necessary to buy bottled water. A good water filter on your faucet or portable water filtration pitchers stored in your refrigerator will eliminate most impurities.

The Eastern Ayurvedic technique of downing 4-8 glasses of water first thing in the morning is said to cleanse your system to help cure and prevent illness. I learned this from a dear Indian friend and try to practice it every day, although I will admit that it sometimes takes me all day to finish my supply! (Hint: Keep your day's supply in one container, so you can measure your progress.)

Drink one glass of water every two waking hours to reach the optimum 6-8 glasses a day.

Eat a diet high in good oils, such as fish, two to three times a week. Cold water fish such as salmon, white tuna, herring, ocean trout, and sardines are high in the omega-3 fatty acid that is said to help prevent cancer by regulating inflammation and cell growth in our bodies.

Limit fat intake, especially the saturated fats found in foods like red meats, butter, cheese, whole milk, cream, and regular margarine, all of which have an unhealthy balance of Omega 6, a fatty acid that causes inflammation. Instead, eat lean meats from animals that haven't been injected with growth hormones or antibiotics. Some studies indicate these chemicals may be helping to fuel today's increase in cancer.

Read the label and consider:
Five grams of fat in a serving are the
equivalent of eating one teaspoon of pure fat. (Yuck!)

Get most of your protein through non-beef sources, such as fish, skinless, broiled chicken or turkey (light meat has less fat), low fat yogurt, hard (less fatty) cheese, tofu, fish, beans, low-fat milk or soymilk. (Note: Breast or prostate cancer patients should first consult their doctor about consuming soy, since it may interfere with their chemotherapy. Non-dairy almond or coconut milk may be acceptable substitutes.)

If you eat meat, it is best to limit servings to no more than 2-3 ounces (about the size of a deck of cards) a maximum of twice a week. Many studies have indicated that a high consumption of meat increases the risk of cancer, especially colon, breast, prostate and lung.[25] Meat from free-range and wild animals is less likely to contain harmful pesticides and hormones. **Avoid cured or smoked meats,** such as hot dogs, bacon, jerky, and ham. Research has linked the nitrates used to preserve these meats to a higher risk of cancer. [26] Be cautious when cooking meats, as cancer-causing compounds are formed in meat that is grilled, well-done, or charbroiled.[27]

Use reduced-fat dairy products, but *not* non-fat. The fat in dairy products has a very high concentration of CLA (conjugated linoleic acid), a fatty acid that has demonstrated anti-cancer properties in laboratory tests.[28] Cheese produced by grass-fed animals has the highest levels of CLA.[29] Again, buy organic products to avoid potentially carcinogenic growth hormones and pesticides.

Use olive or canola oil instead of butter, margarine, shortening, corn or vegetable oil, which are sources of trans-fatty acids. Buy unrefined, expeller- or cold-pressed oils. These retain more nutrients, which are destroyed by heat processing. Never overheat oils, as the chemical change can be carcinogenic.

Eat whole grain breads, rice, and cereals, avoiding baked goods made with white flour. Whole grains are metabolized more slowly than refined grains, thus producing less inflammatory insulin. Plus they contain more nutrients and provide natural fiber to cleanse your digestive system.

Some individuals are sensitive to gluten, a substance in wheat that can cause inflammation in the digestive tract. I highly recommend reading the book *Dangerous Grains* by Dr. James Braly, to understand the potential effect of gluten on your health. Dr. Braly claims that gluten sensitivity or intolerance may account for many human allergies and illnesses, including cancer.

Although I haven't been tested for gluten intolerance, my nutritionist suggested giving it up, along with dairy products, which contain casein, a substance with properties similar to gluten. After just three months of not eating gluten and casein, I not only rid myself of chronic digestion problems, but I also lost ten pounds without dieting. Weight gain or loss is often how the body signals us that something in our diet has been causing it distress, perhaps even dangerous inflammation. I don't plan to resume consumption of gluten or casein products any time soon. Check with your doctor or nutritionist to see if a gluten-free diet is right for you.

Avoid refined sugar and sweetened soft drinks, which spike blood sugar and cause inflammation, cancer's "food." Even the natural carbohydrates in fruit should be eaten in moderation and consumed with protein to balance blood sugar levels (apple slices and low-fat cheese, for example, or yogurt and bananas).

Eliminate or limit alcohol consumption. Although the phytochemicals in red wines and dark beers have been shown to have some beneficial effects on health,[30] there is also an association between alcohol consumption and many forms of cancer, such as breast, colon, liver, and throat.[31] Alcohol is metabolized into highly reactive compounds that act as free radicals and can damage DNA. The recommended limits are a maximum of 8 oz of wine, one beer, or one ounce of alcohol a day.

Drink plenty of green tea, which contains polyphenols called catechins. The Epigallocatechin gallate (EGCG) contained in green tea is one of the most powerful agents for blocking angiogenesis, or the growth of cancer.[32] I sip a cup of organic green tea throughout the day. Caffeine-free is best, but I admit to indulging in a caffeinated version, since I don't drink coffee.

Take probiotics, important bacteria that help stabilize the intestines to best absorb nutrients from food and get rid of cancer-causing toxins. You can get these through supplements and from cultured milk products, such as yogurt, buttermilk, and Kefir (a fermented form of goat or coconut milk). Foods such as apples, onions, garlic, and broccoli also help maintain the proper balance of these bacterial flora in the intestines.

Keep salt intake low and potassium intake high. A high sodium, low-potassium diet increases the risk of cancer, particularly esophageal and colon cancers.[33] These nutrients should be consumed in proper balance, with a ratio of five times as much potassium as sodium. Most Americans, however, significantly reverse that ratio, consuming less than half as much potassium as sodium. Solutions not only include avoiding high sodium canned foods and soups and not adding table salt to food, but also eating a diet high in fruits and vegetables, which generally have potassium/sodium ratios of at least 50:1. Especially good ratios are found in bananas, oranges, and potatoes, to name a few.

For additional information on a cancer prevention diet, including recipes, grocery lists, and menus, read *A Dietician's Cancer Story*, by Diana Dyer, MS, RD, or check her website at www.*CancerRD.com.*

Organic - To Buy or Not to Buy?

Organic foods are those that are grown without the aid of synthetic pesticides and fertilizers, resulting in safer food containing more healthy nutrients. They are typically more expensive, and, hence, may cause you pause at the grocery store. A bag full of organic produce may feel more like a bag full of gold when you leave the checkout counter.

Watching for sales and coupons is one way to minimize food costs while maximizing health. Many health food stores will feature cost-saving coupons on their websites or in their newsletters and in-store fliers. Another way to budget your grocery list is to focus your organic purchases on those products most likely to contain concentrations of pesticides. These include most meats and dairy products, since pesticides are stored in animal fat.[34]

The fruits and vegetables most likely to be contaminated are those with thin or no skins, such as apples, berries, cucumbers, peppers, celery, and lettuce. Some of the least contaminated choices include onions, melons, blueberries, bananas, and oranges, among others. Peeling or washing the skins of fruits and vegetables reduces exposure. Soak the item in a mild solution of additive-free soap such as Ivory or pure Castile soap, or use an all-natural vegetable wash that can be found in the produce section of most stores.

Exercise

Exercise in various forms can do much to improve a cancer patient's well-being both during and after treatment. Not only does it lessen fatigue and stress, but it also enhances immune system function. Some studies show that regular exercise can significantly reduce the risk of cancer, cutting overall cancer risk nearly in half.[35] In fact, one report says that women who exercise regularly reduce their risk of getting breast cancer by up to 60 percent compared to women with low levels of activity.[36]

Recent research also indicates that physical activity plays an important role in helping cancer survivors avoid a recurrence of cancer.[37] Even during cancer therapy, exercise can be one of the best medicines. Just a moderate walk around the yard or block can stimulate your immune system and elevate your mood.

On the other hand, some suggest that *over*-exercising could have the opposite effect for certain types of cancer. The best advice is to consult your doctor before beginning any new exercise regimen. Then begin slowly, and stay within the boundaries of your ability and any restrictions related to your treatment.

In addition to its wellness benefits, exercise may also help fend off a serious decline in physical fitness that can last long after therapy has ended. According to Dr. Wendy Demark-Wahnefried of the University of Alabama, in just one year of chemotherapy, breast cancer patients may replace enough muscle tissue with fat to equal the effects of ten years of regular aging. This means that a 45-year-old would develop the weaker, fatter body of a typical 55-

year-old. Vanity, if not health concerns, would likely lead most cancer survivors to aim for the recommended 2-1/2 hours of exercise each week.

My body tells me when it needs exercise. I feel what I call "krinky," or sluggish, and in need of the increased blood flow and oxygen to my muscles that stretching and moving bring. Every morning I must do my Yoga stretches before I can function effectively, and a run indoors on the treadmill or, weather permitting, outdoors is essential for getting blood flowing to my brain. It is also a good way for me to meditate and plan my day as I focus on my surroundings and get into "the zone."

Outdoor exercise is usually preferable, if not always practical. Nutritionists recommend sunlight as the best source for getting our daily doses of Vitamin D (At least 15 minutes in the sun is worth 3,000 to 10,000 IUs (International Units) of a Vitamin D supplement, more than ten times the recommended daily amount (RDA).[38] In addition to the weather, however, air quality is a consideration when determining whether indoor or outdoor exercise is healthier.

If a propensity for exercise is not implanted in your DNA, then you may have to find incentives. Walk your dog, sign up for an exercise class (Tai Chi is a gentle way to get started.), or find a friend to exercise with you. Then determine the time of day that you are most likely to stick to your exercise regimen. (For me it's morning. I'm likely to put it off toward the end of the day when I am busy.) One way or another, get moving!

A good exercise program should include all three major forms of exercise: stretching, strengthening, and cardiovascular.

Cardiovascular: This is generally defined as an aerobic form of exercise that you can sustain for several minutes or longer. Examples include walking, cycling, swimming, and dancing.

Walking at a moderate pace for at least 15 minutes several times a week may be the best approach for beginning a cardiovascular exercise program. If you were relatively sedentary prior to cancer treatments, you may wish to begin your exercise program slowly, concentrating on exercising regularly in small bits of time instead of trying to break speed or distance records.

Strength training: The benefits of strength training to a recovering cancer patient are many: In addition to increasing overall fitness, it can help rebuild tissues and body functions weakened by the effects of the cancer and treatments. It builds stronger bones, improves immune function, promotes better balance and coordination, and improves one's sense of well-being.

Strength training may either involve lifting weights or participating in resistance exercise. The latter includes squats, push-ups, leg lifts, or any type of body movement that pits your muscles against gravity. As with cardiovascular exercise, you should begin slowly and gradually increase the amount and intensity of exercise over time. The recommended number of sessions is no more than two or three a week, to allow the muscles to recover and rebuild.

After therapy, I noticed a marked decline in leg strength that became especially apparent whenever I squatted down to reach items on the lower shelves of stores. I felt twice my age as I pushed myself up with a grunt and sigh. Exercising weekly with weights has made a big difference in my ability to move, and I can now bounce up with ease again.

Stretching: Stretching not only increases flexibility, but also enhances agility and balance. Some milder forms of stretching include Tai Chi and beginning Yoga. Some say that cardiovascular and strength exercises are more important than stretching;

however, stretching enhances the effects of the other two. Plus it can be done easily at home, even before you get out of bed. I find that morning bed stretches are essential to getting my blood circulating and allowing me to wake up. Stretching increases the blood flow and oxygen supply to the areas of the body that are stretched. I usually stretch several times a day, especially when I've been sitting for a while.

For more information on exercising during and after cancer treatments, I recommend   Dr. Julie Silver's book, *After Cancer Treatment: Heal Faster, Better, Stronger,* from which I gathered much of the above information.

Breathing

Breathing is essential to life. And, like life, we often take this amazing act for granted. Breathing is reflexive from the moment we take our birth gasp. But from then on we often forget to indulge in it properly, breathing shallowly and stingily most of the time. Oxygen is free, if not always pure, so we really should stop rationing it in our bodies. Deep, slow breaths provide benefits that we may not realize, reducing stress and strengthening our cells.

I use daily habits as reminders to breathe properly. Each time I sit down at the computer, dinner table, and even in the doctor's office, I make a point to assess my posture and breathing. My goal is to align my backbone with my head as if a string were pulling me upward from the top of my head, like a puppet. Then I take at least one large breath into the depths of my diaphragm, hold it for a second and slowly exhale through my lips, aware of the flow of air through my windpipe, nose, and mouth. I integrate this miniature meditation into my movements several times a day and I recommend that you do the same.

Sleep

I have always been a big fan of sleep, and never one to rise perky from slumber. In fact, I consider morning people to be annoying, especially when they behave cheerfully before I've even pried open my second eyelid. Unlike our little dog Yogi, who used to bound into my bedroom each morning, full of energy and excitement, I am not a "morning dog." I appreciate the value of sleep.

My somnolent perspective is vindicated by studies on the health advantages of a good night's sleep. *Prevention Magazine* has cited several studies showing that sleep deprivation (less than eight hours a night) may be linked to health risks such as heart disease, depression, anxiety, high blood pressure, and Type 2 diabetes. Even slight amounts of sleep deprivation cause the body to release stress hormones that produce harmful inflammation in the blood system.[39] A healthy immune system needs to be fortified with sleep, and the traditional eight hours is still the suggested minimum.

Getting adequate sleep is especially important while undergoing treatments. Therapy and medications may make this an easy task. If not, the natural sleep aid Melatonin can help. Naps are good, too. The essential ingredient in maintaining health during and after cancer treatments is to allow your body time to repair and recharge through rest and relaxation.

Environmental and Other Toxins

More than 1.2 billion pounds of pesticides and herbicides are sprayed or added to food crops each year in the U.S., equaling five pounds for each man, woman, and child.
(*How to Prevent and Cure Cancer Through Natural Medicine*)

Research has shown certain environmental factors to be potentially carcinogenic, such as pesticides in our food, electromagnetic fields (EMFs) from cell phones, and some chemicals in toiletries. In fact, a US government cancer panel recently highlighted the growing body of evidence linking environmental toxins to cancer, and it warned that Americans are facing "grievous harm" from unregulated chemicals in the air, food, and water. The panel notes that government regulations have been inadequate to protect consumers, whose exposure to multiple chemicals (approximately 80,000 currently in commercial use) over a lifetime may result in cancer. It said recent studies have even found industrial chemicals in the umbilical cord blood of developing fetuses![40]

Shortly before publication of this book, polyethylene glycol (PEG), a chemical present in everyday products such as cleaners and soda pop, was linked to an abnormally high number of bird deaths near Denver wastewater treatment plants.[41] Another study detected a controversial chemical, bisphenol-A (BPA), in the urine of an estimated 93 percent of Americans, possibly absorbed through the skin of those touching the ink on receipts from supermarket and automated teller machines.[42] Dangerous toxins are all around us and, short of living in a sterile bubble (which would probably be made of another toxic chemical!), we can't avoid them all. What we can do is fortify our body's defense system against these potential invaders.

Since the evidence is not always conclusive regarding the effects of various environmental toxins on cancer, I encourage you to check out the research and make your own decisions. There are many books on the subject, but the two I found most helpful are *Anti-Cancer* and *How to Prevent and Cure Cancer with Natural Medicine*. Both of these take a critical look at the internal and external exposures that have been shown to increase cancer risk in contemporary society, some of which are summarized below.

Household products. Suspected carcinogens permeate almost every aspect of our daily lives—from the chemicals used in common household cleaning products to the unpronounceably long chemical perchloroethylene/tetrachloroethylene used in dry cleaning our clothes; and from household insecticides to the parabens, phthalates, and aluminum used in personal hygiene products and cosmetics. Even the way we cook can be dangerous: Scratched Teflon pots and pans may contaminate food, and PVCs may seep into foods and liquids heated in plastic containers or Styrofoam.

What can we do? The easiest solution is to buy natural or organic products, which are becoming increasingly available in even the most traditional stores. "Green" cleaning products can be found in most grocery stores, as can paraben-free cosmetics, natural toothpastes, and aluminum-free deodorants, to name a few. I always read the labels carefully, especially for products that will be applied to my skin, ingested, or inhaled. If the label looks like a pharmaceutical dictionary, I will often pass up the item in favor of a product with fewer syllables in its ingredients list.

Cosmetics and personal hygiene products. Since these products are likely to be used every day and directly applied to the body, they merit particular attention. Antiperspirants may be of particular concern for women, because they usually contain the moisture barrier aluminum, a suspected carcinogen that some scientists have linked to breast cancer. Plus the aluminum may be absorbed into the body more easily when women shave their armpits. Since I have not yet found an anti-perspirant without aluminum, I decided to use a natural deodorant and try not to perspire too much!

Perfume. As almost all perfumes contain phthalates, the only way I know to avoid this exposure is to go without perfume, or to use its less potent cousins, cologne and toilet water, which contain fewer phthalates. It is easier to avoid the phthalates and parabens in cosmetics and hair care products. Natural cosmetic companies, such as Aveda, Body Shop, and Origins, have proliferated in recent years, featuring a wide selection of nontoxic beauty products.

Hair dyes. Some scientists and natural health care practitioners believe that the chemicals in hair dyes may be carcinogenic. Because these products are usually applied to the hair roots, they are easily absorbed into the scalp, which has a rich blood supply capable of transporting toxins throughout the body. Dark colored, permanent dyes are of special concern, due to a higher concentration of chemicals. Bleaching agents have not been proven to be carcinogenic, nor have the nonpermanent vegetable-based dyes or henna.

EMFs. There is disagreement about whether the electromagnetic fields (EMFs) from cell phones, microwave ovens, telephone transmitters, and other electronic devices are harmful to health. Although recent tests have shown a possible connection between cell phone use and certain brain tumors, there is no definitive proof at this point. Little research has been done on microwave ovens or food cooked by them, but some studies have shown changes in the properties of microwaved food that could affect the immune system.

Lacking conclusive evidence for either the safety or danger of EMFs, I land somewhere in the middle on this topic. I heat some foods and liquids in the microwave, but I stir-fry, bake, steam, and eat raw foods as much as possible. When operating a microwave, I stand at least three feet away. And I have always shied away from living near power lines or microwave towers.

I am most cautious when it comes to cell phones, given studies showing a possible link to brain tumors. On this issue, I have definitely decided to err on the side of caution. I have chosen to follow recommended precautions (See page 108.), and I suggest that others consider doing the same.

Staying Strong

Those who have experienced a life-threatening illness in themselves or a loved one are particularly vulnerable to emotional stress even after the illness has abated. Despite our elation over finally getting through treatments and being "cured," we retain a lingering feeling of vulnerability. The emotional veil of taking life for granted has been lifted.

Experts warn that the grief process cancer patients go through after diagnosis is often cyclical, and it may return in smaller doses each time we go in for diagnostic tests or maintenance treatments. Nothing changes the tone of my day more quickly than the call from my oncologist's office to set up my next MRI—except perhaps going in for the MRI itself. Although I convince myself that things will continue to be okay, I always feel that small finger of uncertainty pressing into my stomach as my husband and I walk down the hall to learn the scan results from my oncologist. A false alarm a few years back remains in the depths of my memory, keeping me ever aware of my vulnerability.

More than most people, we cancer survivors know that we are not in control of our fate, and our psyches are permanently etched with that awareness. But we are also survivors, and that spirit helps us prevail.

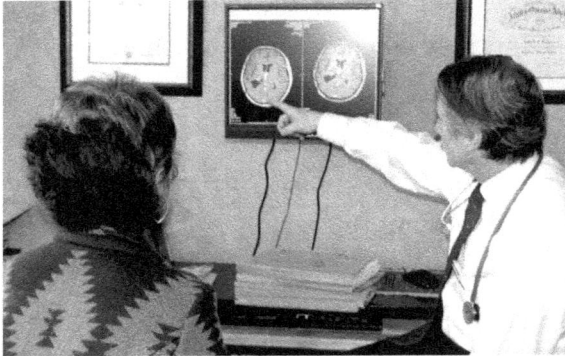

Going over MRI results with my oncologist, Dr. Edward Arenson

Anticipation

(Waiting for MRI results, by Lyn Densem- Chambers, April 2009)

Anticipation.
 Waiting, wondering.
Soon the known will meet the unknown.
The now will meet the future,
 uncertain, unsure.

Newly disgorged from the machine—the cold,
 clanking machine that maps my fate
 on a black and white screen—
I am still waiting, wondering,
 searching the doctor's face as he passes by.

Does he know?
>Or is he waiting and wondering, too?

I anxiously attempt to blend into a painting on the wall,
>>where gold light flows
>>>into a darkened cave,
>>>like knowledge into the unknown,
>>>>warmth into uncertainty.

>>A divine ray of hope,
>>the light follows me down the hall
>>into the doctor's darkened office,
>>>its color soon forfeited to the
>>>>harsh blue light of the computer's eye,
>>>where the future is revealed
>>>>in stark shades of grey,
>>>>in skeletal images that morph
>>>>into patterns at the doctor's command
>>>>too quickly,
>>>>too starkly,
>>>>too darkly to understand.
>>>>>What? What?

>>>As images flash before my eyes,
>>>>the doctor explains
>>>>cautiously,
>>>>calmly.
>>The unknown becomes known,
>>>>and there's no more waiting,
>>>>wondering

>>>>for now.

Moving On

The most important factor in moving on productively with the gift of life we survivors have been given is knowing how to deal with negative stress in a positive way. Chapter Five enumerates several ways to deal with stress through techniques such as meditation, exercise, massage, and more. As our lives pick up pace after treatment ends, stress-reducers are as important as ever to maintaining a healthy immune system.

Stress-reduction Reminders

- **Don't push yourself.** Avoid getting back into unhealthy patterns of over-booking your life.
- **Write down your "to-do" list** and check things off as you complete them. Spread them out to different dates on your calendar, allowing plenty of time to finish each one.
- **Breathe deeply and slowly.**
- **Stop and notice** small moments of beauty and humor.
- **Take catnaps** when needed.
- **Have a massage,** acupuncture, warm bath, or Jacuzzi regularly.
- **Delegate and accept help.** Trying to be everything to everyone is a major source of stress.
- **Stop and switch to another activity** for awhile when you start to feel stressed.
- **Avoid negative people and situations.**
- **Meditate.**
- **Get fresh air and exercise.**
- **Eat regularly and nutritiously.** (Skipping meals can be stressful to your body.)
- **Spend time with friends and family.**
- **Participate in enjoyable activities on a regular basis.**

Preventive Screening

For those of us already diagnosed with cancer, regular screenings may be built into our future. Even if they aren't, it is important to keep tabs on this aspect of our health. My husband still wonders if I could have caught my tumor earlier by following his advice to check on my headaches many years ago. And we both wonder whether his mother's early death from breast cancer and my aunt's premature departure due to stomach cancer might have been avoided or postponed with early detection and treatment.

Early cancer detection is critical to staying well. Regular exams and screenings for all kinds of cancer are highly recommended. A summary of American Cancer Society Recommendations follows. Check with your insurance company about coverage, as some insurance companies have different timetables. Most of all, stay aware of your body and any changes in its appearance or behavior. Enlist a friend, spouse, or partner to help you inspect areas you may not easily notice on your own, such as the skin on your back or the top of your head. Then act on any suspicions by scheduling a doctor visit without delay. Time may be the critical factor that saves your life.

American Cancer Society Screening Recommendations

- **Breast cancer**. Clinical exams about every three years for women in their 20s and 30s; yearly mammograms and clinical exams starting at age 40; self-exams for all women on a daily basis. Talk with your doctor about your history to see if you should have additional tests at an earlier age. For more information, contact the American Cancer Society and ask for the document, *Breast Cancer: Early Detection.*

- **Colorectal cancer**. Beginning at age 50, flexible sigmoidoscopy every 5 years, or colonoscopy every 10 years; Yearly fecal occult blood test. Talk with your doctor about your history and what colorectal cancer screening schedule is best for you. For more information, contact the American Cancer Society and ask for the document, *Colorectal Cancer: Early Detection.*

- **Cervical cancer.** All women should begin cervical cancer screening about three years after they begin having vaginal intercourse, but no later than 21 years old. Screening should be done every year with the regular Pap test or every two years using the newer liquid-based Pap test. Some women, because of their history, may need to have a different screening schedule for cervical cancer. Please see the ACS document, *Cervical Cancer: Early Detection* for more information.

- **Endometrial (uterine) cancer.** At the time of menopause, all women should be informed about the risks and symptoms of endometrial cancer. Women should report any unexpected bleeding or spotting to their doctors. Some women, because of their history, may need to consider having a yearly endometrial biopsy. Talk with your doctor about your history.

- **Prostate cancer.** Starting at age 50, talk to your doctor about the pros and cons of testing so you can decide if testing is the right choice for you. If you are African American or have a father or brother who had prostate cancer before age 65, you should have this talk with your doctor starting at age 45. For more information, please see the ACS document, *Prostate Cancer: Early Detection.*

- **Cancer-related check-ups.** For people aged 20 or older having periodic health exams, a cancer-related check-up should include health counseling and, depending on a person's age and gender, exams for cancers of the thyroid, oral cavity, skin, lymph nodes, testes, and ovaries, as well as for some non-malignant (non-cancerous) diseases.

For more detailed information, check *www.cancer.org* or call your local American Cancer Society.

Precautions for Cell Phone Use
Adapted from Anti-Cancer[43]

• **Keep the cell phone as far as possible away from the body**, even when not in use. The strength of the EMF is four times lower at four inches, and 50 times lower at three feet.

• **Use a speaker phone or a hands-free device**, such as a wireless Blue Tooth headset. Text messaging is preferable, as it limits proximity to the body and is usually of shorter duration.

• **Stand away from anyone using a cell phone**, and avoid using one in close quarters, such as a subway or a bus, where you can expose others to the EMFs from your phone.

• **Use the "flight" or off-line mode** to stop EMF emissions when not in use.

• **Avoid carrying a cell phone next to your body** regularly, even on stand-by (which still emits signals).

• **If you do carry a phone, position the keyboard toward your body** so the antenna, which emits the strongest signals, faces away from you.

• **Choose a phone with the lowest magnetic field** or SAR (specific absorption rate). Rankings of most cell phones can be found on the Internet. Check *www.fcc.gov*.

• **Keep conversations short,** calling back on a corded landline for longer conversations. (Cordless phones use microwave technology similar to that of a cell phone.)

• **Switch ears frequently** and keep the phone away from your head while connecting, when signals are strongest.

• **Avoid using a cell phone when traveling in a vehicle**, as EMF strength is greatest when the phone continually attempts to connect to new transmission antennae. A hands-free system such as Bluetooth still emits EMFs, but signals may be weaker depending on the distance of the antenna from your body.

Journal entry one year after treatment ended (sitting on the deck of our mountain cabin, where it all began.):

I feel my body, my self, coming back to me. Slowly but surely, like the morning sounds that herald the awakening of the day—birds clattering for food, the soft hush of the breeze through the trees, and the whir of car ignitions nearby as humanity interjects its presence. I feel stronger and ready to plunge into the flow of reality. Lessons learned, I recall James Baldwin's quote: "If you know from where you came, there is no limit to where you can go." I'm ready to go again!

Planning a New Future

As mentioned earlier, being "in the moment" is a powerful tool for surviving during the difficult times after diagnosis, as well as for thriving every day. However, most of us also need to look to the future to sustain our mental and emotional well-being. Goals and plans bolster our psyches and keep us moving forward. This is just as true, if not more so, for cancer patients. Whether planning for a trip after the next round of treatments, or looking toward returning to one's job, you can benefit both emotionally and physically from having goals.

Of course, each year of wellness and survival is a goal in itself. Yet getting there can also be an important part of the trip. Within your larger goals are the components of rebuilding your physical and emotional health. In her book, *After Cancer Treatment*, Dr. Julie Silver discusses how to set wellness goals:

1. **Decide what you want to accomplish** (increased strength, stamina, more time with friends, daily meditation, etc.), and write it down.

109

2. **Prioritize your goals**, determining which are the most important to accomplish first, second, etc. Some may be short-term goals (within a few weeks), and others long-term (6-12 months or more).

3. **Decide how you will measure your progress** in reaching each goal (for example, be able to run a mile a day), and be realistic (perhaps walk a mile first).

4. **Identify any obstacles** that might impede your progress, such as lack of motivation or energy.

5. **Enlist support** from individuals and resources to help you reach your goals (consider a walking buddy).

6. **Check your progress regularly**, adjusting your goals and activities as necessary.

Living Life with No Regrets

> *Unfold your own myth.*
> *-Rumi*

Besides physical goals for regaining and maintaining your health, it is important to have emotional goals connected to realizing your dreams. When faced with life-threatening illnesses, we suddenly think about our unfulfilled dreams and wonder if we will have time to realize them now that life has presented us with a potential boundary. When we are well, we tend to put things off to the endless tomorrows we take for granted. Cancer can be a motivator to start accomplishing our goals and experiencing our desires without further delay. Now is the time to get serious about those Someday Dreams.

Did you always want to learn to fly? travel to the Rainforest? act in a play? What have you thought about doing when you retire? Perhaps now is the time to do it instead of waiting. *Carpe Diem!* Put something fun and exciting in your goals.

Here are a few hints for discovering your deep, inner goals: Determine what you value most in life (people, animals, nature, for example) and what you most enjoy doing every day (such as cooking, singing, reading, playing sports). What have you always wished you could do more often if you had time? (Volunteer, paint, build something, fish, travel, etc?).

Sometimes discovering our inner dreams may be as simple as observing what we naturally gravitate to when left to our own devices. We usually do what we love, not what we think we should love. For me, it is writing. I thought it was painting, because I enjoy that, too. But when I look at what I naturally do--even in my head before I get up in the morning—it is crafting words, writing. For others it may be singing, dancing, or doodling.

Ask yourself what you would regret not doing when you finally move on to the beyond. This is a good question for everyone, whether or not they have faced a serious illness.

For some people the answer may involve adventurous endeavors, such as climbing a mountain or competing in a marathon. For others, it might be as commonplace as learning to draw, to play an instrument, or starting a business. If you're not sure, many books can help you define your goals, including Dr. Silver's. With proper planning, even individuals with heavy workloads related to family and jobs can find time for Someday Goals.

My Someday Goals are both mundane and adventurous. Most of all, I want to spend more time with friends and family, commune with nature's eternal soul in my favorite places on the coast and in the mountains, and, once I have grandchildren, to play a significant role in their lives. I also want to travel to exotic places such as Thailand and Sicily: to continue making a difference in cross-cultural understanding; and to realize my childhood dream of writing books that are meaningful, as I hope this one is.

I have already started to accomplish my Someday Goals. I went to Sicily last fall and had the time of my life. Thailand is next on my list. And, if you find this book helpful, I can check off another goal and move on. I wish the same for you. Stay healthy, have fun, and never forget to live life fully, from the inside out!

Look to this day and enJOY!

A poem I wrote about realizing my creative dreams... (Note: Scientists say the right side of the brain is where creativity resides, while the left side is more analytical and linear. I have always tended to be more left-brained, and have admired those whose lives are lived more on the right side. The tumor left a space on my right side that I hope to fill with more creativity!)

Right Brain, Left Brain

We are the doers who plod headlong into the day,
answering to the click, the beep, the ring.
Creating charts, and plans, and programs,
a network that binds us together like a web,
and moves us to the next day.

We drive, work,sleep,walk into the ether of
a reality we have created to survive, to prosper, to do.

We search for the next signpost to say we have arrived.
At where, we do not know, but we know it is s*ome*where,
and that is what counts, works, functions,climbs,dives,
succeeds, or fails in a limp handshake with life.

They are the dreamers who give us the hush to discover what lies in the
quiet of our minds. the push that inspires, and the fire to see beyond the
veil of everyday to someday.
To create, to build, to be.
 To plumb our rusty souls.
 To take life by the hand and skip through mind meadows
 lush with possibilities, and brilliant with colors that make mortal eyes
blink.
They are the Artists,
And we,the Artisans.

  -Lyn Densem-Chambers, 6-09

Life Inside Out

Appendix

Daily Wellness Reminder*

- Breathe deeply
- Laugh frequently
- Stretch and exercise regularly
- Appreciate each moment
- Pray or meditate every day
- Sleep at least 8 hours, nap, and relax
- Eat healthy foods
- Drink 6-8 glasses of water
- Avoid environmental toxins
- Do something meaningful
- Plan a healthy future
- Smile and laugh often
- Have fun, and do what you love!
- Personal others:

* *Cut this out and post it someplace where you'll see it regularly. Add your personal goals next to each reminder and at the end.*

Energy Builders

When you discontinue therapy you may find your blood counts diminished, along with your energy level. Here are some tips for perking yourself up as you rebuild your system:

Green tea: Sip throughout the day, with bag left in cup, and/or take green tea capsules at regular intervals during the day.

Vitamin B capsules also promote energy and can be taken several times throughout the day, as directed on the bottle.

Frequent stretching and light exercise (such as walking inside or outside): This is particularly helpful if you are stationary most of the day.

Fresh air: Go outside at least a couple of times a day for several minutes at a time--to the mailbox, a neighboring office, house, or around the block. Even a short breath of fresh air on a porch or deck can be invigorating.

Cat naps: A short nap or rest can re-start your engine. Each person may differ on the amount of time needed for a refreshing rest, but many experts recommend between 15 and 30 minutes. Longer naps can take you into REM and leave you groggy. Avoid taking naps close to bedtime, which could result in poor nighttime sleep.

Lyn's Morning Energy Smoothie

Blend together:

    ¼ cup liquid Mangosteen

    1 T greens powder

    1 scoop protein powder (There are many types to fit your needs and taste.)

    6-8 oz low-fat yogurt, milk, or milk substitute*

    2-4 ice cubes

    1 cup fresh or frozen fruit (blueberries, banana, strawberries, raspberries, etc., according to preference)

    1 T ground flax seeds (adds a slightly nutty taste)

    1 T fish or flax oil, with the proper balance of Omega 3 and 6

    (Optional) If desired, add artificial sweetener, to taste. (I recommend Stevia Extract, a natural herbal sweetener with zero calories.)

Note: Most of these products can be found at health food stores, if not your local grocery store. Check with a nutritionist or health food expert for further information.

* Breast or prostate cancer patients should check with their doctors about using soy. Dairy alternatives to soy products include those made with rice, almond, and coconut.

Recommended Reading

Braly, James, and Ron Hoggan (2002). *Dangerous Grains: Why Gluten Cereal Grains May be Hazardous to Your Health.* New York: Penguin Putnam, Inc. A very informative book exploring the impact of wheat, rye, and other grains on a range of health conditions, including cancer, autoimmune diseases, osteoporosis and intestinal diseases, among others.

Buckman, Robert (2006).*Cancer is a Word, Not a Sentence: A Practical Guide to Help You Through the First Few Weeks.* Buffalo, New York: Firefly Books. A six-step guide for navigating cancer diagnosis and treatment.

Carr, Kris (2008). *Crazy Sexy Cancer Survivor.* Guilford, Connecticut: Morris Publishing group. A humorous and inspirational guide to living life as a cancer survivor.

Chopra, Deepak (1989). *Quantum Healing: Exploring the Frontiers of Mind/Body Medicine.* New York: Bantam Books. An endocrinologist schooled in Western medicine, Dr. Chopra explores ancient Eastern methods of healing that focus on the role of the mind, such as Ayurveda, meditation, Yoga, and other alternative approaches. A fascinating and provocative must-read for anyone interested in holistic health.

Dyer, Diana (2007). *A Dietitian's Cancer Story.* Ann Arbor, Michigan: Swan Press. A practical guide on healthy nutrition for those experiencing and recovering from cancer.

Dyer, Wayne W. (2004). *The Power of Intention: Learning to Co-create Your World Your Way.* Carlsbad, California: Hayhouse, Inc. A process for attracting what you want into your life, with approaches for staying positive through illness and treatments.

Healy, Bernadine (2007). *Living Time: Faith and Facts to Transform Your Cancer Journey.* New York: Bantam Dell. A physician's thoughts on treatment, both physical and psychological, based on her own experience with cancer.

Krohn, Jacqueline, and Frances Taylor (2000). *Natural Detoxification.* Vancouver, Canada: Hartley and Marks. An encyclopedic guide to natural methods of detoxifying the body.

Ireland, Karin (2004). *Learning to Trust Myself: Lessons from Cancer and Other Life Dilemmas.* Austin, Texas: Wise Words Publications. Using her personal journey with breast cancer, the author discusses treatment alternatives and encourages readers to pay attention to the signals in their own bodies and to trust their instincts when it comes to care.

Kubler-Ross, Elizabeth, and David Kessler (2008). *On Grief and Grieving: Finding the Meaning of Grief through the Five Stages of Loss*. New York: Scribner. An explanation of the process of accepting illness, death, or other major losses.

Murray, Michael, Tim Birdsall, Joseph E. Pizzorno, and Paul Reilly (2002). *How to Prevent and Treat Cancer With Natural Medicine.* New York: Penguin Group. A reference on alternative medicines and nutrients to prevent, treat, and cope with the side-effects of cancer and cancer treatments.

Omartian, Stormie (1999). *Just Enough Light for the Step I'm On: Trusting God in the Tough Times.* Eugene, Oregon: Harvest House Publishers. A religiously-based book on how to get through times of difficulty one step at a time. It contains suggestions that even the non-religious may find helpful.

Sark (1998). *Make Your Creative Dreams Real: The Bodacious Book of Succulence. New York:* Simon and Schuster. Or check out other books by Sark (She just goes by one name.) She writes fun, colorfully presented books on how to stimulate creativity and joy in life. Cure your soul and cure your body!

Scovel Shinn, Florence (1989). *The Wisdom of Florence Scovel Shinn.* New York: Simon and Schuster. The collected works of this longtime metaphysician and lecturer features affirmations and quotes to help with healing and overcoming difficulties in life.

Servan-Schreiber, David (2008). *Anticancer: A New Way of Life.* New York: the Penguin Group. A research-based treatise on the causes and remedies for cancer, with information on how to stay healthy.

Silver, Julie K. (2006). *After Cancer Treatment: Heal Faster, Better, Stronger.* Baltimore: The Johns Hopkins University Press. Written by a doctor and cancer survivor, this book provides a step-by-step plan for helping cancer patients get and stay healthy.

Tolle, Eckhart (1999). *The Power of Now.* Vancouver, Canada: Namaste Publishing. A guide to happiness that focuses on learning to appreciate the moment. Perhaps a bit "heady" if you're not feeling well, but the message is certainly worth the reading.

Online Resources:

www.cancer.org. (The American Cancer Society site) Provides information and resources for cancer patients and their families. Supports research, patient services, early detection, treatment, and education. Also a good first resource for checking out wigs and other head coverings to deal with hair loss.

www.cleaningforareason.org. An international nonprofit that provides free housecleaning services to chemotherapy patients once a month for up to four months.

www.dol.gov/ebsa/faq_compliance_cobra . Answers questions about health benefit provisions under the Consolidated Omnibus Budget Reconciliation Act (COBRA), which allows continuation of insurance coverage that otherwise might be terminated when leaving an employer-provided health plan.

www.ssa.gov/disability . Provides information and application forms to apply for Federal Disability Insurance for those who cannot work during illnesses or other disabilities.

Personal Medical Information

Your name: _____ Contact phone: _____

Emergency contacts:
Name:_____Phone:_____Relationship:_____

Doctors:
Oncologist: _____Phone:_____

Radiation therapist: _____ Phone: _____

Primary care physician: _____

Phone: _____

Other: _____ Phone: _____

Insurance:
Company: _____ Group #:_____

ID#:_____ Phone: _____

Medical Information:
Surgeries (types/dates):_____

Major illnesses/conditions:
_____

Drug or other allergies:
_____

Medications:
Prescription drugs (name/strength/dosage):
_____

_____

Vitamins and other supplements
(name/strength/dosage):_____

_____

Other information:

References

Preface

1 Boyle, Peter, et al, "2008 World Cancer Report, International Agency for Research on Cancer," Journal of the American Cancer Institute (9 December 2008); vol 100: 1672-1694.

Chapter 1: My Story

2 www.cancer.org/Research/CancerFactsFigures/indexhttp://emedicine.medscape.com/article/283252-overview.

Chapter 2: Dealing with Diagnosis

3 Kubler-Ross Elizabeth and David Kessler, On Death and Dying (New York: Scribner,1969).

4 Mattison, D., "The Forgotten Spirit: Integration of Spirituality in Health Care,"USA.Nephrol News (February 2006), 20(2),30-2.

5 "Dark chocolate: Half a Bar Per Week May Keep Heart Attack Risk at Bay," Science Daily (24 September 2008).

Chapter 3: Making Decisions

6 Pam Stephan, How to Choose the Right Oncologist: Be Observant, http://www.about.com//breast cancer/od/lifetimeduringtreatment/qt/choose_doctor.htm About.com. Accessed September 28, 2006.

Chapter 4: LIVING through Therapy

7 Chemo Brain, http:// www.cancer.org/treatment/treatmentandSideEffects/PhysicalSideEffects/ChemotherapyEffects/Chemobrain. Accessed July 26, 2010.

8 Ibid.

9 Ibid.

10 Darshan, Archana, Go Ahead and Take Cat Naps,<http://ezinearticles.com/?Go-Ahead-and-Take-Cat-Naps&id=3508843>. (Accessed 8 March 2010.).

11 "With Cancer, Let's Face It: Words Are Inadequate," Well Blog, New York Times, 15 March 2010.

Chapter 5: Staying Strong To Get Well

12 Tsong, T.Y., "Deciphering the Language of Cells," Trends in Biochemical Sciences 14:89, 1989.

13 Strojonovich, L., et al, "Stress as a Trigger of Autoimmune Disease "Autoimmun Rev. 2008 Jan;7(3): Epub Nov 29 2007.http://www.ncbi.nlm.nih.gov/pubmed/18190880. Accessed 3 October 2010.

14 . Ibid.

15 "27 Ways Pets Can Improve Your Health," Web MD. 9 July 2009. http://pets.webmd.com/slideshow-pets-improve-your-health.

16 Lipton, Bruce H., "Toward a New Noetic Science,"Science, Belief. 11 April 2010.

17 Lipton, Bruce H., "Toward a New Noetic Science,"Science, Belief. 11 April 20.

Chapter 6: A New Beginning: Staying Healthy After Treatment Ends

18 Sevier, Laura, "Cancer and How to Avoid it. Interview with Dr. Servan-Schreiber," The Ecologist. 29 May 2009.
http://www.theecologist.org/green_green_living/health_and_beauty/269374/cancer_and_how_to_avoid_it.html .

19 Ibid.

20 Servan-Shreiber, David, Anticancer: A New Way of Life, (New York: Viking Press, 2008), p. 44.

21 Murray, Michael, Tim Birdsall, Joseph E. Pizzorno, and Paul Reilly, How to Prevent and Treat Cancer with Natural Medicine (New York: Penguin Group, 2002), p. 4.

22 Servan-Schreiber, Anti-cancer, p.48.

23 Ibid., p.67

24 Ibid., p.99

25 Murray, Op Cit., p. 36.

26 Murray, Op. Cit., p. 44.

27 Ibid., p.78.

28 Dyer, Diana, A Dietitian's Cancer Story. (Ann Arbor Michigan: Swan Press, 2007), p. 24.

29 Murray, Op. Cit.,p. 69.

30 Dyer, Op Cit., p. 21.

31 Murray, Op. Cit., p. 37.

32 Servan Schreiber, Op. Cit., p. 102.

33 Jansson B. Potassium, Sodium and Cancer: a review. Journal of Environmental Pathology Toxicology and Encolorgy 1996:15:65-73. (From Anti-Cancer, p.

34 Murray, Op. Cit., p. 35.

35 Murray, Op. Cit., p. 35.

36 Ibid.

37 "Cancer Survivors Should Exercise, New Guidelines Say," The Denver Post. 6-29-10.

38 Sun Exposure to the Skin is the Human Race's Natural, Intended, Most Effective and Most Neglected Source of Vitamin D,"Sunshine Vitamin. Org. http://www.sunshinevitmin.org. 7 May 2010.

39 "Twenty-eight Days to a Healthier Heart," Prevention.com. 2-17-2010.
http://www.prevention.com/28daystoahelathyhert/5.html

40 Layton, Lindsey, "Risk of Chemicals 'Underestimated,' Experts Say," The Washington Post, as reported in The Denver Post, 7 May 2010.

41 Horn, Sarah, "Chemicals Play a Role in Metro Duck Die-offs," The Denver Post, 28 July 2010.

42 Layton, Lindsey, "Disputed Chemical Turns up in Receipts," The Washington Post, as reported in The Denver Post, 27 July 2010.

43 Servan-Schreiber, Op. Cit., p.207-208.

www.ingramcontent.com/pod-product-compliance
Lightning Source LLC
Chambersburg PA
CBHW022306060426
42446CB00007BA/633